DARLINGTON TO NEWCASTLE

via Durham

Roger R Darsley

Series editor Vic Mitchell

 Middleton Press

Front Cover picture: A4 class 4-6-2 no.60016 Silver King *justifies the class nickname of 'Streaks', as it storms through Plawsworth station with an up express train. This was 5th April 1952 and the last day that Plawsworth was open to passengers. (J.W.Armstrong Trust)*

Rear Cover picture: In 1960, The Railway Correspondence and Travel Society persuaded BR to repaint the station pilots at York and Newcastle in NER lined green. Class J72 0-6-0T no.68723 is shunting the carriage roads between the main departure platforms, 8 and 9, at Newcastle Central station on 12th September 1960. (R.R.Darsley)

Rear Cover map: Railways of the area in 1921 with closed and subsequent stations added.

Readers of this book may be interested in the following societies:	North Eastern Railway Association www.ner.org.uk
Head of Steam - Darlington Railway Museum Station Road, Darlington, DL3 6ST www.head-of-steam.co.uk (Home of the Ken Hoole Study Centre)	North Eastern Locomotive Preservation Gp www.nelpg.org.uk
Darlington Railway Preservation Society Station Road, Darlington, DL3 6ST http://drps.synthasite.com/	The Robert Stephenson Trust www.robertstephensontrust.com
	Railway Correspondence and Travel Society, NE Branch rcts.org.uk/branches/branch-nea-north-east/
The A1 Steam Locomotive Trust Darlington Locomotive Works Hopetown Lane, Darlington, DL3 6RQ www.a1steam.com	Friends of the Stockton & Darlington Railway www.sdr1825.org.uk

Published April 2007
First reprint February 2020
Second reprint March 2023

ISBN 978 1 904474 98 2

© *Middleton Press, 2007*

Design Deborah Esher

Published by
    Middleton Press Ltd
    Camelsdale Road
    Haslemere
    Surrey
    GU27 3RJ
Tel: 01730 813169
Email: info@middletonpress.co.uk
www.middletonpress.co.uk

The 200th Anniversary of the Stockton & Darlington Railway is to be celebrated in 2025. A remodelling of Darlington Bank Top station will be seen by then, along with a new £20m visitors' centre at Darlington North Road.

Printed by Mapseeker Digital Ltd, Unit 15, Bridgwater Court, Oldmixon Crescent, Weston Super Mare, North Somerset, BS24 9AY.   Telephone +44 (0) 01922 458288 +44 (0) 7947107248

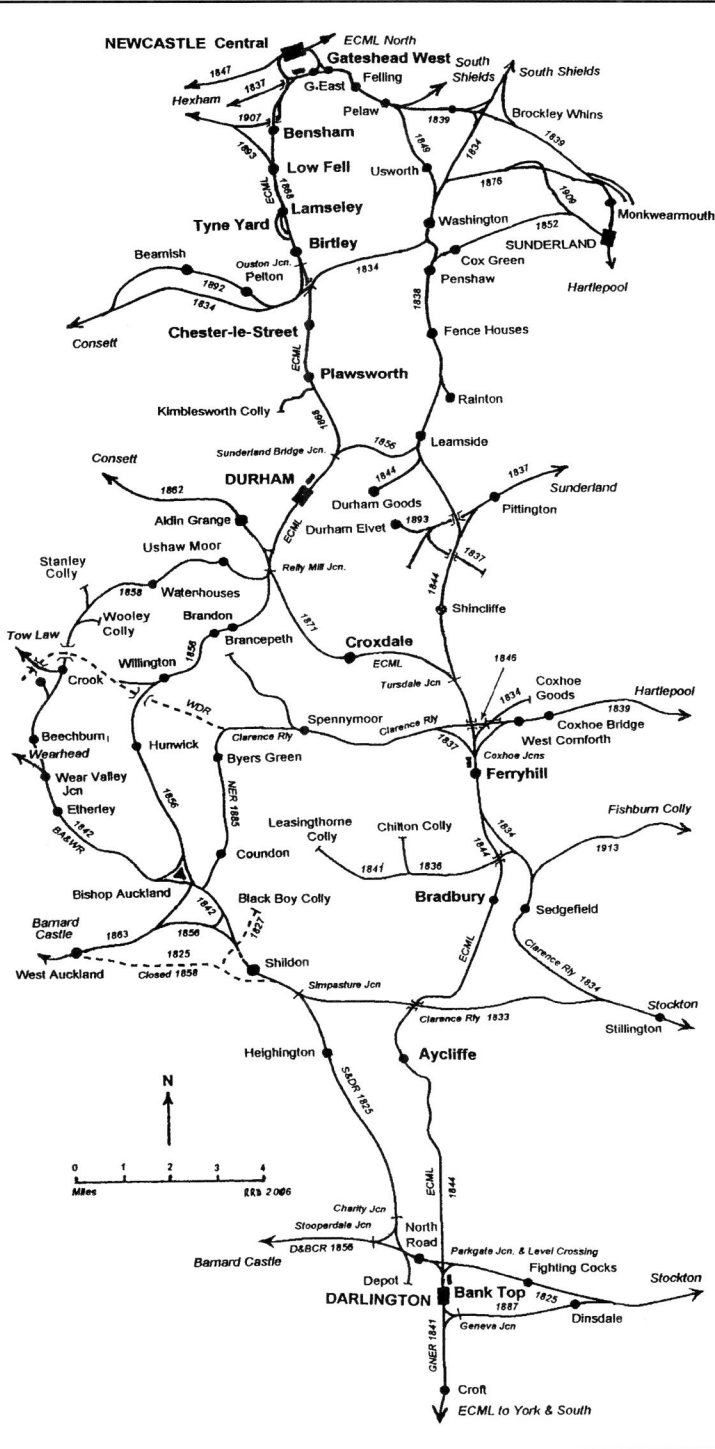

CONTENTS

23	Aycliffe
100	Bensham
84	Birtley
27	Bradbury
75	Chester-le-Street
44	Croxdale
2	Darlington Bank Top
47	Dearness Valley Junctions
54	Durham
31	Ferryhill
103	Gateshead West
92	Lamesley
95	Low Fell
111	Newcastle Central
82	Ouston Junction
71	Plawsworth
	Robert Stephenson & Hawthorns Ltd:
112	Forth Banks
20	Springfield
89	Tyne Yard

I. Railways of the area in 1921 with closed and subsequent stations added.

ACKNOWLEDGEMENTS

No book like this can be researched and written without the help of local experts, professional archivists, and enthusiasts like myself. My thanks go to those who are acknowledged in the photographic credits and to D. G. Charlton, G. Croughton, N. C. Langridge, S. Lockwood, V. Mitchell, Dr. J. Rainbow, P. J. Robinson, A. Thompson, D. Tyreman, as well as to M. Grout at the Ken Hoole Study Centre, J. L. Harrop at Beamish Museum, A. C. Clothier and M. Brown at the Robert Stephenson Trust, K. Williamson at Darlington Borough Library, and staff at the Durham Record Office and Newcastle City Libraries. As always, my special thanks go to my wife, Norma, for secretarial assistance – and much forbearance.

GEOGRAPHICAL SETTING

Our line crosses the County of Durham from south to north. The county is defined by three major rivers. The Tyne borders the north and the Tees the south. The River Wear, like the Tees, drains down from the highlands of the Alston Block in the Northern Pennines.

Underlying the county is the Great Northern Coalfield which was the cradle of the Industrial Revolution. The coal was laid down as a continuous sheet of carboniferous sediment from 1½ft. to 10ft. thick. In the west of the county these seams came to the surface and were the best quality coal. These were mined first and the problem was the great cost of getting the coal to navigable sections of the three rivers.

First the waggonways, and then, after the Stockton and Darlington Railway of 1825, the railways produced in Durham a pattern of coal exporting lines from the west to the east. This conflicted with the strategic communications of the country going south to north between the centres of population.

The tilted plateau of the Alston Block is composed of Millstone Grit and Limestone, with three main mineral faults running through it. This area of the county was mined for lead and quarried for limestone. Associated shales were a source of iron ore, which, together with the coal and lime, gave rise to a large iron and steel industry.

County Durham became, in the 19th and 20th centuries, one of the most industrialised and urbanised parts of the country. In 1866 County Durham was supplying half the world's coal and one third of Britain's iron. Yet by 1993 all the collieries had gone as had most of the steelworks. Durham County Council has engaged in a determined policy of reclamation, so most of the county has reverted to a sylvan outlook.

These 37 miles of the East Coast Main Line start at Darlington on the River Skerne, a tributary of the Tees. As the line goes north, it breaches the limestone ridge at Ferryhill and crosses the River Wear and its tributaries before following the valley of the River Team to cross the deep and steep banks of the River Tyne at Newcastle. This required eight impressive viaducts and two high level bridges across the Tyne.

The maps in this volume are scaled at 25 inches to 1 mile and are dated 1921-1922 unless otherwise stated. North is at the top unless indicated differently.

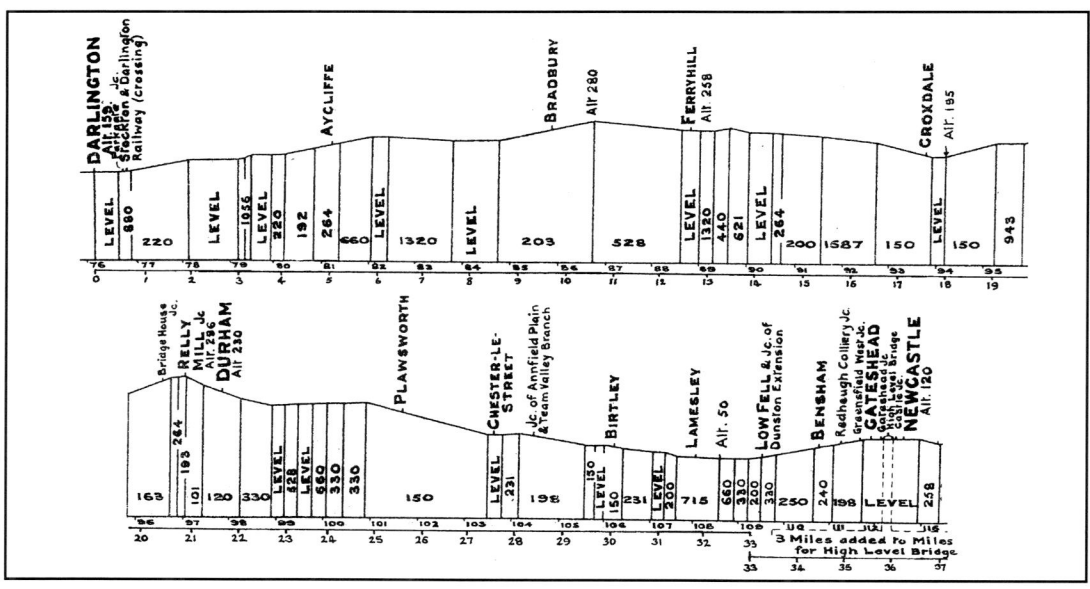

HISTORICAL BACKGROUND

The Stockton & Darlington Railway (S&DR) of 1825 passed north of Darlington with North Road station at Hope Town, though there was a siding to Darlington depots. A competitor running to the north and roughly parallel to the S&DR, was opened in 1833. It was named after the popular Duke of Clarence (later King William IV). It diversified with a branch to the city of Durham and reached Ferryhill where they cut a laborious but important cutting through the limestone ridge in 1835. This done, the Clarence Railway was financially broken and could go no further.

In 1829, the S&DR built a branch to Croft via Bank Top, Darlington, to provide an interchange for Yorkshire trade and coal going south across the border. In 1834, the Act for the Sunderland and Bishop Auckland via Durham railway had been passed. This was another 'coal to the sea' railway. Also proposed in 1834 was a line that was effectively the route of the present East Coast Main Line (ECML), but this was not to happen for many years.

In the Railway Mania of the 1840s there was a race to get the first line from London to Edinburgh. The Great

North of England Railway (GNofER) built a line from York to Darlington which opened on 30th March 1841. It entered Bank Top using part of the S&DR Croft branch but the GNofER had no money to go further north.

This was where George Hudson, a York entrepreneur, nicknamed the 'Railway King' entered the scene. He organised the Newcastle & Darlington Junction Railway (N&DJR) in 1842 and with characteristic briskness, built it by 1844. To do this, he grabbed every available bit of existing railway that might get him there quickly, even if it was circuitous. His route was from Darlington Bank Top north to Ferryhill. The line crossed the River Skerne many times and on Bradley Carrs the track had to be laid on a wooden base and mound to stop it sinking into the marshy ground. At Ferryhill he made use of the Clarence Railway cutting to head north as far as Rainton Crossing. Robert Stephenson then told him to obtain control of the Durham Junction Railway (DJR), the Pontop & South Shields Railway (P&SSR) and the Brandling Junction Railway (BJR). The DJR was to run from the Stanhope & Tyne Railway (S&TR) at Washington station crossing the River Wear at Fatfield by the Victoria Viaduct. The construction of this viaduct had run the DJR out of money. The S&TR had also massive financial problems and the P&SSR was its eastern section. The BJR also connected with the S&TR. Hudson rescued these lines from their financial concerns. He combined them into a larger N&DJR and saved himself a lot of track building. This made it possible to get to Gateshead via Leamside, Brockley Whins and Pelaw. He built an elegant station at Greenesfield in Gateshead, while everyone paused to consider the crossing of the River Tyne.

Hudson formed the York & Newcastle Railway (Y&NR) on 3rd August 1846 by merging the N&DJR with the GNofER. The Newcastle & Berwick Railway across the River Tyne was amalgamated with the Y&NR on 9th July 1847 to form the York, Newcastle & Berwick Railway (YN&BR). But in the Spring of 1849 Hudson's devious financial dealings came to light and he was forced to resign. The High Level bridge across the Tyne and the Newcastle Central station were under construction by then and Queen Victoria and Prince Albert performed the ceremonial openings on the way to their holiday in Deeside. Heading south the Queen opened the bridge on 28th September 1849 and heading north on 29th August 1850 they both opened the still unfinished station.

On the 31st July 1854, the YN&BR was amalgamated with the York & North Midland Railway, the Leeds Northern Railway and the Malton & Driffield Junction Railway to form the North Eastern Railway (NER). This railway company then went on to become one of the country's most formidable and efficient regional monopolies.

The NER began in 1862 to construct the more direct route that forms the current ECML. This Team Valley route went south from Gateshead the 14 miles to Newton Hall junction north of Durham. It was opened for goods on 2nd March 1868 and for passengers on 1st December 1868. At Newton Hall junction the line joined the Sunderland to Bishop Auckland via Durham line, which, proposed in 1834, had not been opened until 1st April 1857. The new route was still inconvenient for through express trains, so a new nine mile link between Durham and Ferryhill was authorised in 1865 and opened on 1st October 1871 for freight and on 15th January 1872 for passengers. The present ECML was then complete.

By the beginning of the twentieth century the NER had quadrupled the tracks from Ouston Junction to Low Fell to deal with the flow of freight traffic to the Tyne. On the 10th July 1906 the new bridge over the river was opened by King Edward VII, which meant the end to reversal in Newcastle for trains to and from Scotland.

In 1923 the NER became a major player in the London & North Eastern Railway (LNER). Although Kings Cross and Doncaster may have become more influential than York and Darlington, many of the commercial and operational practices of the NER were sound and lasted until Nationalisation in 1948.

The line was first in British Railways, North Eastern Region. That then became part of a larger Eastern Region on 1st January 1967 and in 1968 British Railways became British Rail (BR). The exhaustion of the Durham coal reserves and the advent of the car had a marked effect on the stations and connections with the ECML. Croxdale, the first station to close, did so in 1938. The village and suburban stations followed in the 1950s, as did some of the feeder services such as Ferryhill to Spennymoor and Hartlepool services. Local freight survived until the 1960s, when there was a wholesale closure of goods facilities and branch lines such as the Bishop Auckland, Waterhouses and Lanchester branches that met the ECML at the Deerness Valley junctions. Advantage was taken to ease the curves where junctions had been and to allow higher speeds. The Deltic class of Co-Co diesel electrics with their characteristic engine sound were introduced in 1961 and were worthy successors to the NER Atlantics and the Gresley Pacifics on this route, as were the High Speed Trains of 1978. It was the ECML electrification project of 1989 that brought regular 125 miles per hour running on the line.

Signalling at Newcastle from 1909 had been converted to electro-pneumatic. In 1959 it was replaced by a centralised signal control box. A mixture of semaphore and coloured lights dating from 1931 was replaced by track circuit block controlled colour light signalling between Darlington and Ferryhill (1967) and between Ferryhill and Durham (1970). On 12th April 1991, as part of the electrification scheme, the whole route came under the Tyneside Integrated Electronic Control Centre (IECC), and signalling became bi-directional with multiple aspect colour light signals and, from 2002, with solid state interlocking.

A belated attempt to modernise freight handling led to the building of a very large marshalling yard at Lamesley in 1963, but Tyne Yard never reached its full potential as the freight moved to road transport. In the 1980s, BR was divided into sectors. In 1987 Trainload Freight from all sectors: aggregates, coal, metals and petroleum were seen on the line. At Privatisation in 1994 all Trainload Freight in the area became Load Haul which was bought by EWS in 1996. In 2006, freight operators likely to be seen on the route were EWS, Freightliner, GB Railfreight and DRS. BR Parcels and Royal Mail went to EWS, which included the mail services to Low Fell. Royal Mail did not renew the contract in 2004. In 1996 responsibility for the track passed to Railtrack, who were replaced on 3rd October 2004 by Network Rail.

Passenger services were prepared for franchising as Inter City East Coast, Inter City Cross Country and Regional Railways NE. Great North Eastern Railway (GNER) won the first seven year term and was perceived to do well. They won the renegotiated franchise in 2005.

Cross Country was taken by Virgin Rail Group and after a slow start, they had with their frequent service of Voyager trains revitalised this section and reconnected stations like Chester-le-Street to the national network. It had been decided to split Cross Country into two new franchises in 2006. Regional Railways NE Ltd was taken by Mersey Transport Ltd (MTL) who branded the services 'Northern Spirit'. MTL was bought by Arriva in 2000 and they changed the brand to Arriva Northern. On 19th October 2004, they lost the new franchise to a consortium of Serco and Ned Railways (the UK branch of Nederlandse Spoorwegen) who operate under the 'Northern Rail' brand. TransPennine Trains were separated out from the Northern Spirit franchise and, in 2004, given to First Group (originally First Bus). In 2006, they introduced new class 185 diesel multiple units to these services.

PASSENGER SERVICES

In 1854, which was the first year of the NER, there were eight up trains and seven down trains between York and Newcastle on weekdays. Two of these trains, each way, had accommodation for 3rd class passengers. The average speed was 39mph for express and mail trains and 22mph for slow or stopping trains. This may seem slow but the proportional advantage these trains had over road transport then was twice that of GNER trains over cars today. However, comparison between the timetables of 1854 and 1866 showed little improvement. These trains would have travelled from Darlington to Ferryhill and then via Leamside. It was not until 15th January 1872 that the East Coast expresses went via Durham and the Team Valley route. The shorter route fed into the timetable, but the spur to faster running came in 1888 when principal day trains on the West Coast route from London to Edinburgh cut the journey time to 9 hours from 10. The East Coast route had been taking 9 hours since 1876. The Great Northern Railway (GNR) took the trains from Kings Cross to York and the NER took the train from York to Edinburgh with a reversal and engine change at Newcastle. The East Coast felt the need to respond and reduced their time to 8½ hours. There then began the railway races of August 1888. In the first fortnight the trains got faster (and lighter). Finally on the 14th, the East Coast time was 7 hours 32 minutes. Neither of the companies really liked these races despite the immense publicity, so they met and fixed the booked times to be 7¾ hours on the East Coast and 8 hours on the West Coast. However, the East Coast could not resist a parting shot and on 31st August did the journey in 7 hours 15 minutes with a six coach, 100 ton train. The average speed was 57.7 mph and from York to Newcastle the train was hauled by a NER Tennant class 2-4-0.

This behaviour was repeated in 1895, but from London to Aberdeen after the Forth bridge had been opened. In 1855 the journey had taken 17½ hours, in 1887, it was down to 14 hours. The best time from the East Coast before the races were halted again was to do the 523½ miles at a speed of 60.4 mph or 61.8 mph excluding stoppages. The 80.5 miles from York to Newcastle was completed in 79 minutes. While York to Darlington includes the NER racing grounds, that time required very good work on the sinuous lines between Darlington and Newcastle. In 1904, the 12.20 Newcastle-Sheffield express hauled by R class (D20) 4-4-0 was claimed to be the fastest train in the British Empire.

Throughout its history the Darlington to Newcastle line has seen some of the country's most famous trains. "Flying Scotsman" was synonymous with the 10.00 am departure from Kings Cross to Edinburgh but it was introduced as a non-stop service from Kings Cross to Newcastle on 1st May 1928. The "Silver Jubilee" express was introduced from September 1935 and "The Coronation" 5th July 1937. "The Elizabethan", introduced in 1953, took over the timings of "The Capitals Limited" between Kings Cross and Edinburgh and was then the longest non-stop passenger train service in the world. This was achieved by using A4 Pacifics with corridor tenders allowing crew changes en route. It ended on 9th September 1961 with the introduction of diesels where crew changes required a stop at York and Newcastle. Other named trains included the Pullman trains, the Glasgow to London "The Tees-Tyne Pullman" and the Newcastle to London "Queen of Scots".

Another train, which like "Flying Scotsman" and "The Elizabethan", travelled the route but did not stop at Darlington, was "The Norseman" from Kings Cross on its way to the Tyne Commission Quay and the Scandinavian Ferries. Overnight "The Aberdonian" and "The Night Scotsman" took the fast lines outside the station but "The Tynesider" stopped. Other named trains on the route to Edinburgh were "The Talisman" and "The Heart of Midlothian", while the 1957 winter timetable had "The Fair Maid from Perth" shadowing "The Tees-Tyne Pullman". 1964 was the start of a new service, "The North Eastern". Other northern named trains included "The Northumbrian" and "The North Briton".

Times of the fastest trains did not improve until well after the end of the World War II. Five percent improvement came with the change from steam to diesel. The first mainline diesel into Darlington was Type 4 D201 on the down "Flying Scotsman" to Newcastle on 21st June 1958 returning on the 5.05pm from Newcastle the same day. Transition from steam to diesel was a process that lasted a number of years with the last scheduled mainline run being class A1 4-6-2 no.60145, *St Mungo*, on a York to Newcastle relief working returning to York on New Year's Eve 1965.

Fifty minutes came off the time from London with the effective use of the Deltics in the late 1960s and a further 30 minutes was saved by the introduction of the High Speed Trains (HST) in 1978. With the coming of the HST, the naming of trains went, apart from "Flying Scotsman", "The Aberdonian", "The Talisman" and "The

Newcastle Executive" which replaced "The Tees-Tyne Pullman". The first electrified service from Darlington to Newcastle was the 14.30 Kings Cross to Newcastle on 10th June 1991. Electrification meant that in 2006, Darlington was 2 hours 20 minutes from London and the fastest intermediate times in minutes between Darlington and Newcastle were; Darlington-Newcastle – 29 (27 up); Durham-Newcastle – 14 (12 up) and Chester-le-Street-Newcastle – 14 (9 up).

The all-stations stopping trains to Newcastle were withdrawn in stages between 4th June 1945 and 5th December 1955, with the really rural and inner suburban stations closing first. From 16th September 1957 diesel multiple units (DMU) took over virtually all local passenger services on the branch lines from Durham and Darlington, but these all closed in the mid-1960s, except the Darlington to Bishop Auckland line. Ferryhill at this time still had six stopping trains in each direction giving direct access to Kings Cross, Leeds, Liverpool and Bristol, so it was a surprise when Ferryhill was closed on 6th March 1967, for, like Chester-le-Street, this station was a local hub with potential for development. Chester-le-Street looked in the 1970s as if it was going the same way, but fortunately local people intervened and saved the situation.

Durham was more established as an InterCity station. The working timetable for 1960 had 20 stopping trains in either direction on weekdays with up to 30 on Saturdays and 12 on Sundays. The extra trains on the summer Saturdays included such exotics as Filey Holiday Camp-Edinburgh, Scarborough-Glasgow (Queen Street), South Shields-Blackpool, Llandudno-Newcastle, Yarmouth-Newcastle and Bournemouth West-Newcastle. These workings reflected all the summer seaside resorts that lost out when the British discovered the Mediterranean sun.

Timetabling in the days of the franchise is even more complex than before. The Monday-Friday, June-December 2006 timetable has 80 down trains stopping at Newcastle. Six of these do not stop at Darlington (all GNER). Of the 74 which stop at Darlington, 63, including all the TransPennine, Virgin and Northern Rail stop at Durham. Seven of the TransPennine, four of the Virgin and all the Northern Rail stop at Chester-le-Street, making 15 trains in all. Of the 74 trains that left Newcastle in the up direction, 18 stopped at Chester-le-Street of which nine were Virgin, 60 stopped at Durham and 67 at Darlington and seven did not stop at Darlington. On a superficial glance this appears to give a lot of unbalanced workings between franchises! The down Virgin trains stopping at Chester-le-Street came from Doncaster, Birmingham, Cardiff and Bristol, but all the up trains originated from Newcastle. The Virgin stops were introduced upon the withdrawal of most of the through Saltburn-Newcastle services on 23rd May 2004.

The GNER brought back some named trains, including "The Scottish Pullman" and "The Tees-Tyne Pullman", but these disappeared in 2005 with the "Mallard" upgrade of their mark IV coaches. This leaves only "The Northern Lights", "The Highland Chieftain" and their signature brand, "Flying Scotsman".

"BRICKS & MORTAR"

1. Darlington in the nineteenth and twentieth centuries was a railway town. It could be said that the railway provided the bricks and mortar of its development. This is reflected in David Mach's 1997 brick sculpture, The Train. This version of the A4 Pacific weighs 1500 tons (181,754 bricks) but does capture some of the essence of steam. Ironically it is at Morton Industrial Park at least three quarters of a mile from any current railway site. (R.R.Darsley)

2. The tower of Darlington Bank Top station is at the top of Victoria Road on the west side of the station and commands the town skyline together with the Market Place clock tower and the flat topped tower of St John's church. In August 2006 the offices were being used by Network Rail and scaffolding was being erected as part of a major restoration of the building. Most people enter the station from the road entrance that rises from Parkgate between the main platforms. (R.R.Darsley)

DARLINGTON BANK TOP

II. This map, at a scale of 6 inches to 1 mile, is from the 1860s and shows the outline of the 1841 station built by the Great North of England Railway at Bank Top. The 'Engine Fitting Shops' became the NER engine shed in 1885. At the junction with the Stockton & Darlington Railway is the GNofER engine shed which is still in existence. Darlington North Road station is at the new suburb of Hope Town and the only sign of the industrial development around Albert Hill is the South Durham Iron Works.

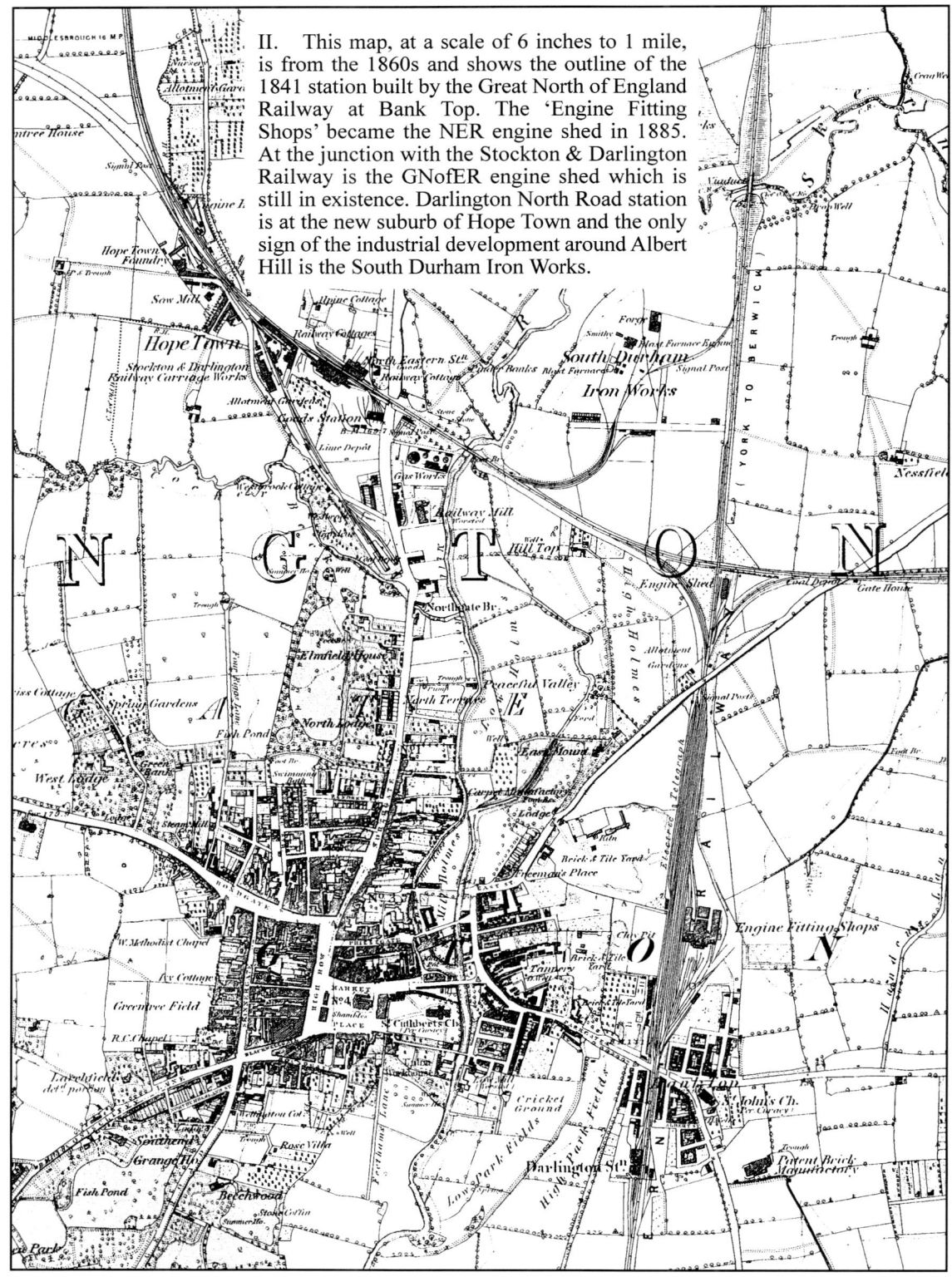

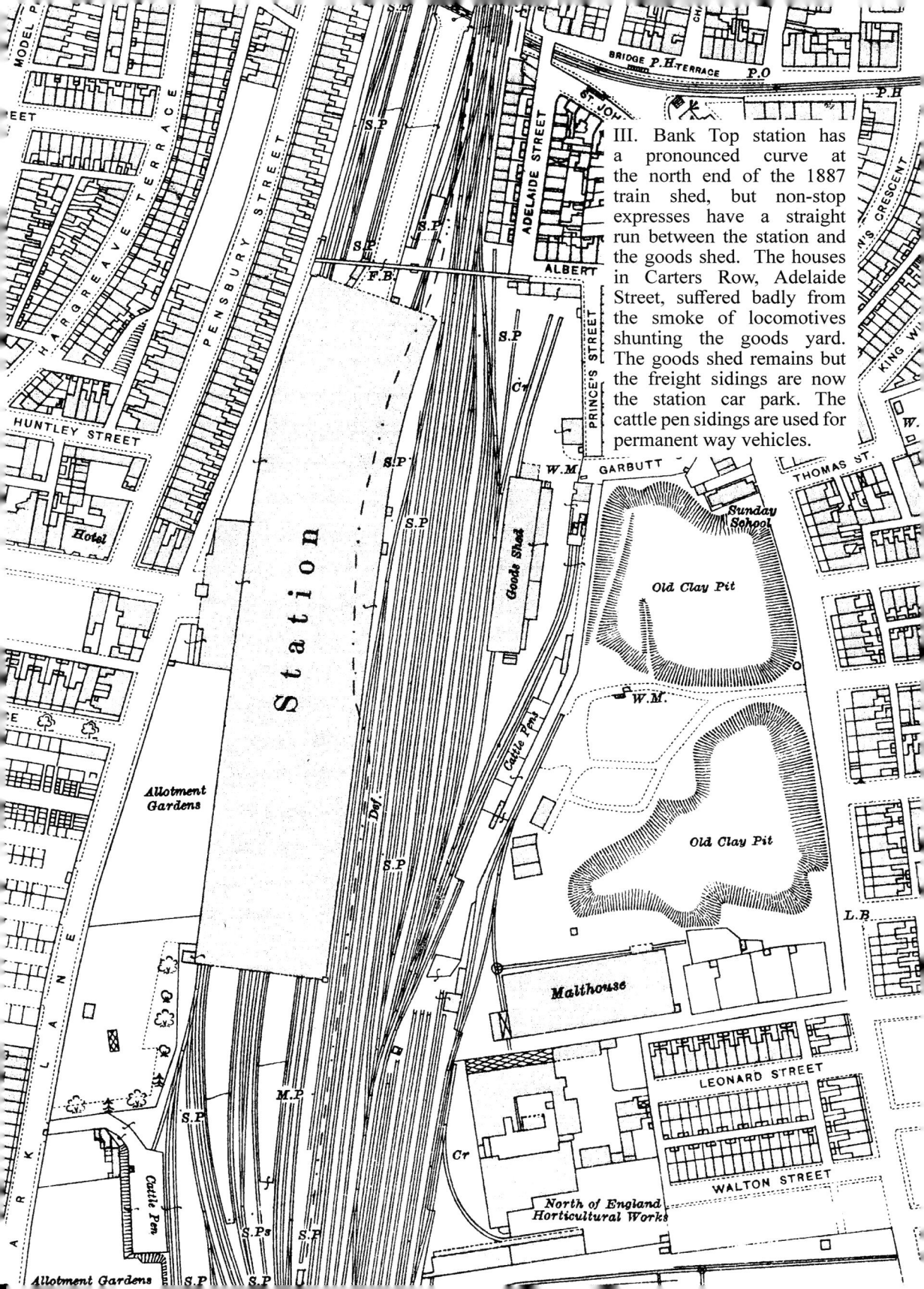

III. Bank Top station has a pronounced curve at the north end of the 1887 train shed, but non-stop expresses have a straight run between the station and the goods shed. The houses in Carters Row, Adelaide Street, suffered badly from the smoke of locomotives shunting the goods yard. The goods shed remains but the freight sidings are now the station car park. The cattle pen sidings are used for permanent way vehicles.

3. The first station at Bank Top, built by the GNofER in 1841, had a simple pitched roof and was known as Darlington NE. It was enlarged in 1863 when it became known as Bank Top. The present station, seen here under construction, was designed by William Bell and completed in 1887. It was the longest arched train shed in Britain until Waterloo International was built in 1992. (K.Hoole coll.)

4. This is the interior of the station in 1899 looking north from the southern end and showing platform 1 for up trains going south. A rake of NER coaches is in the carriage sidings. The main station offices and waiting rooms are in the centre beyond the bay platforms. It appears that passengers were not permitted to spoil the artistic poses of the staff! (Beamish Museum)

5. The northern end of the platform pointed towards the engine shed. An LNER steam railcar is coming off shed. The LNER had 85 of the Sentinel Cammell steam railcars and a further ten Claytons. They were in service from 1925 to 1948 and the majority were named after horse drawn mail or stage coaches. Shildon shed had five to operate the Darlington to Tow Law service and in 1933 Darlington Bank Top shed took over the Darlington to Richmond workings. The original livery was vermillion and cream, but from 1930 this was changed to green and cream. (K.Hoole coll.)

6. Platform 1 in 1955 has plenty of passengers waiting for a London train. Litter on the tracks was as much a problem then as it is today. LNER suburban coaches await their next turn of duty. (Stations UK)

7. Class A4 4-6-2 no. 60013 *Dominion of New Zealand* arrives with a Glasgow to Kings Cross train on 25th July 1958. A J72 0-6-0T is the north end station pilot. Carters Row has been demolished, and Railway Terrace plus Silver Street have been replaced by wartime 'prefabs'. In the background are the water tower and coaling stage of the engine shed. Beyond the Darlington North signal box was the new diesel multiple units stabling area. (R.Leslie)

8. Class A3 4-6-2 no.60075 *St. Frusquin* leaves platform 4 with a special from Scarborough to Newcastle on 14th July 1962. Platforms 5 and 6 were the northern bay platforms for trains to Bishop Auckland, Tow Law, Middleton in Teesdale and Stainmore. The lone enthusiast may be noting the cleanliness of the locomotive, which was fitted with a double chimney in August 1959. (L.W.Rowe)

9. Sixteen years later the signalling has been modernised and one iconic class of locomotive has been replaced by another. Deltic no.55009 *Alycidon* leaves with the 9.00am Kings Cross to Edinburgh train. It is 26th August 1978 and BR blue and grey livery is the norm. However, the Bishop Auckland class 101 DMU has coaches in different liveries. A bus stop shelter has been built for branch line passengers, who for years had stood in the rain. Now both platforms 5 and 6 have been filled in to extend the station car park. (T.Heavyside)

10. Electrification brought greater speed to the ECML in the form of class 91 locomotives and class 82 Driving Van Trailers. The GNER 13.23 to Newcastle awaits a late departure on 1st August 2006. The locomotive is no. 91118 *Bradford Film Festival* and the DVT is no. 82223. The advent of privatisation has brought more trains to the station. (R.R.Darsley)

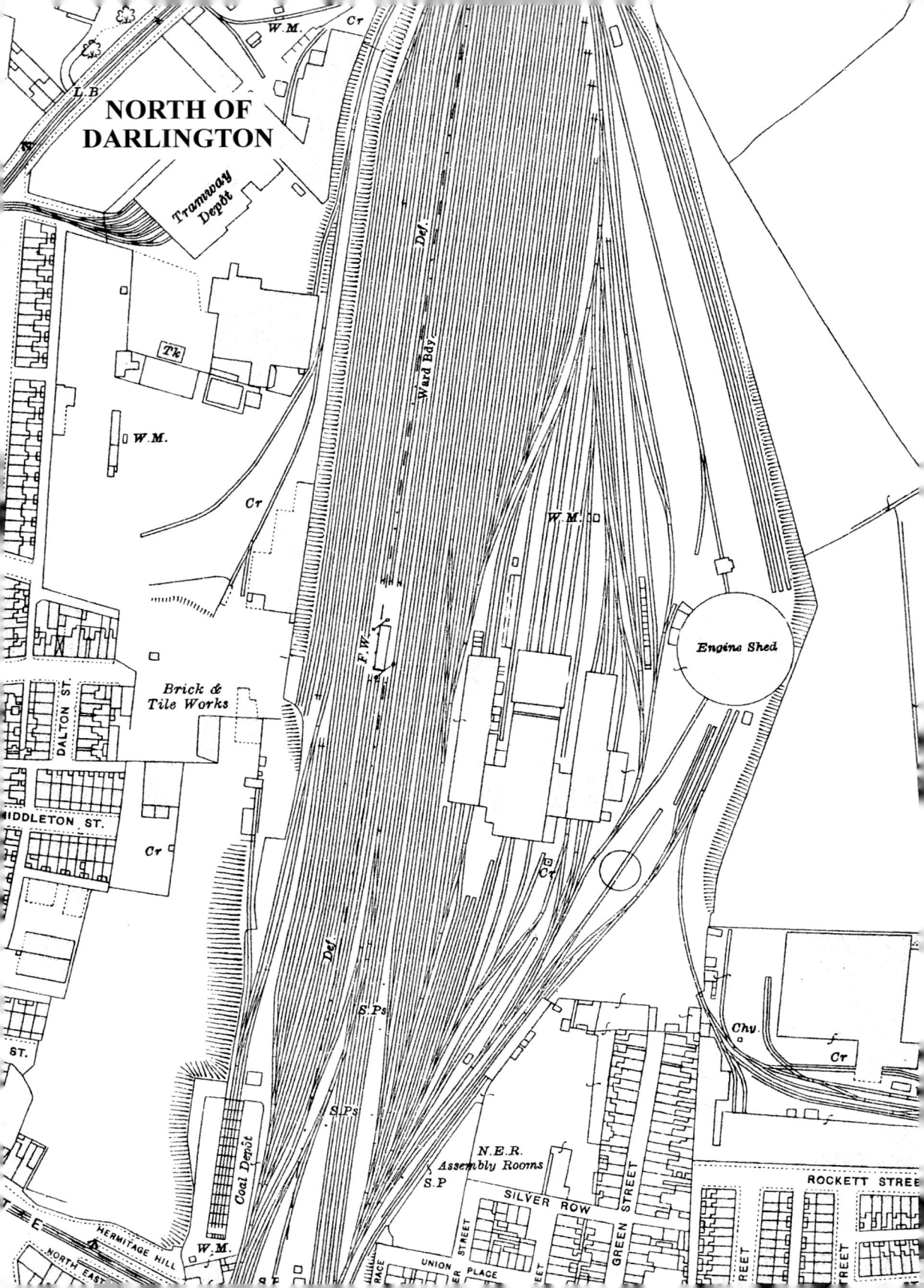

← IV. North of the station were carriage and freight sidings. The original wagon works became the main locomotive shed on 19th February 1885, when the wagon works moved to Shildon. The S&DR engine shed at North Road was closed. This was done for the opening of the new Bank Top station in 1887. The NER added a roundhouse, but in 1939 the shed was rebuilt as a long straight shed with a mechanised coal loading tower. On the west of the railway was the Darlington Power Station and the Tramway Depot.

11. Immediately north of the platforms are the Parkgate road underbridges. Old photographs show sheep and cattle being herded up the road under these bridges. Single deck trolley buses waited for station passengers, as do the buses today. There is now a direct bus service from the station to Durham-Tees Valley Airport. Class 2MT 2-6-2T no.84029 was the last of the class and was the last steam locomotive to be built in the Darlington North Road works. In May 1957 it went into service at Ramsgate and was withdrawn in June 1964. Here it crosses the bridge towards the shed. In the background is Darlington North signal box and the shadow of the Darlington Power Station. (J.W.Armstrong Trust)

12. Darlington shed was coded 51A in BR days and the turntable was at the south end of the shed. The 'thunderbird' locomotive of its day was positioned on a siding to the turntable so that, when duty called, the locomotive could be turned to its correct direction. Class A3 4-6-2 no. 60040 *Cameronian* awaits its call on 14th July 1962. No. 60040 was rebuilt with a double chimney in October 1959 and with German trough style smoke deflectors in March 1962. (L.W.Rowe)

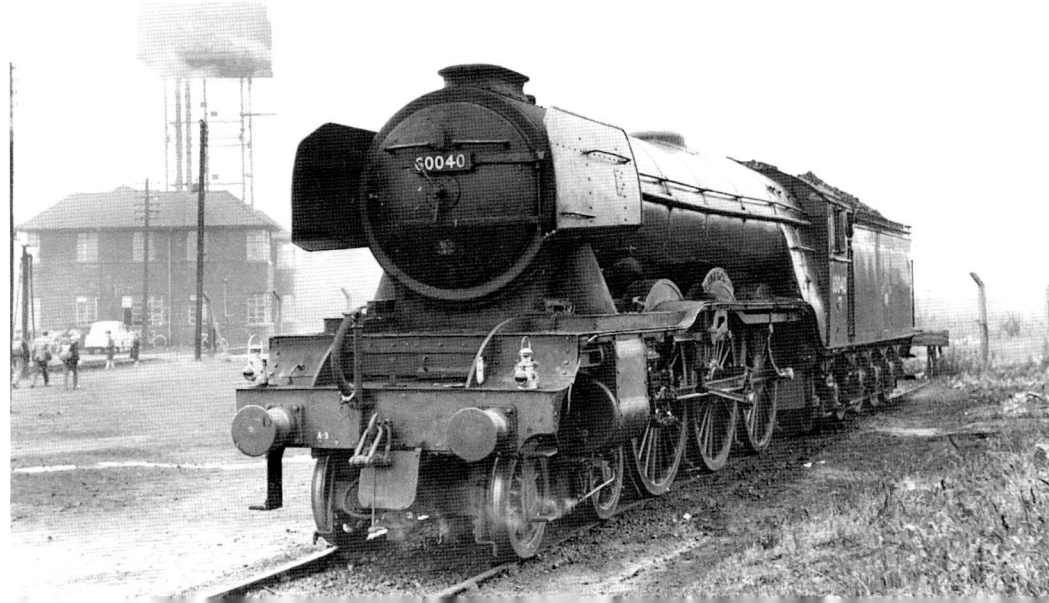

13. The rebuilt Darlington shed is viewed in LNER days from the top of the coaling stage. In the background is the station tower. There are not many locomotives in the yard, but those identifiable are: J27 0-6-0 no.1047, B16 4-6-0 no.926, Q7 0-8-0 no.902, J77 0-6-0T and A5 4-6-2T. Protruding from the shed itself is a Great Northern designed C1 4-4-2 that has worked through from York on 2nd October 1940. (LNER/K.Hoole coll.)

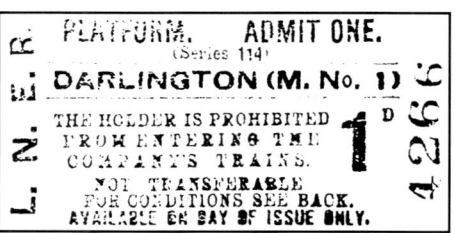

Other views of Darlington can be seen in the Middleton Press album, *Darlington - Leamside - Newcastle* **and** *Shildon to Stockton.*

14. The interior of the shed, probably on the same day, shows on the left J77 0-6-0T no.1344 and a B16 4-6-0. On the right is Q5 0-8-0 no.655, a J21 0-6-0 and a C6 4-4-2. The centre road has one of the class A5 4-6-2Ts built for the LNER Northern Division. (LNER/K.Hoole coll.)

15. In BR days the coaling stage hosts two J71 0-6-0T locomotives; no.68235, no.68279 and two J72s (with smaller wheels). At the end of the line is a J94 0-6-ST, the BR version of the wartime Austerity tank. A B1 4-6-0 is moving up to the water column and in the background is the shed building. The shed closed on 27th March 1966. (E.E.Smith/K.Hoole coll.)

16. Darlington North signal box has gone, but the power station is present though being dismantled. The steam shed has also gone though the diesel multiple unit depot is on the left. No. 25130 has arrived with the Heaton-Manchester (Red Bank) vans. No. 31287 is on a rake of Blue Circle cement hoppers. The date was 26th August 1978. (T.Heavyside)

17. Another favourite vantage spot is Haughton Road bridge, to the north of the shed area. The station tower shows above the DMU depot which opened in 1957 (Code DN). The majority of the class 101 DMUs were in the short lived light grey and blue stripe livery. No. 40121 is on northbound mixed freight while in the distance a High Speed Train is on the mainline heading towards Bank Top on 24th July 1980. (T.Heavyside)

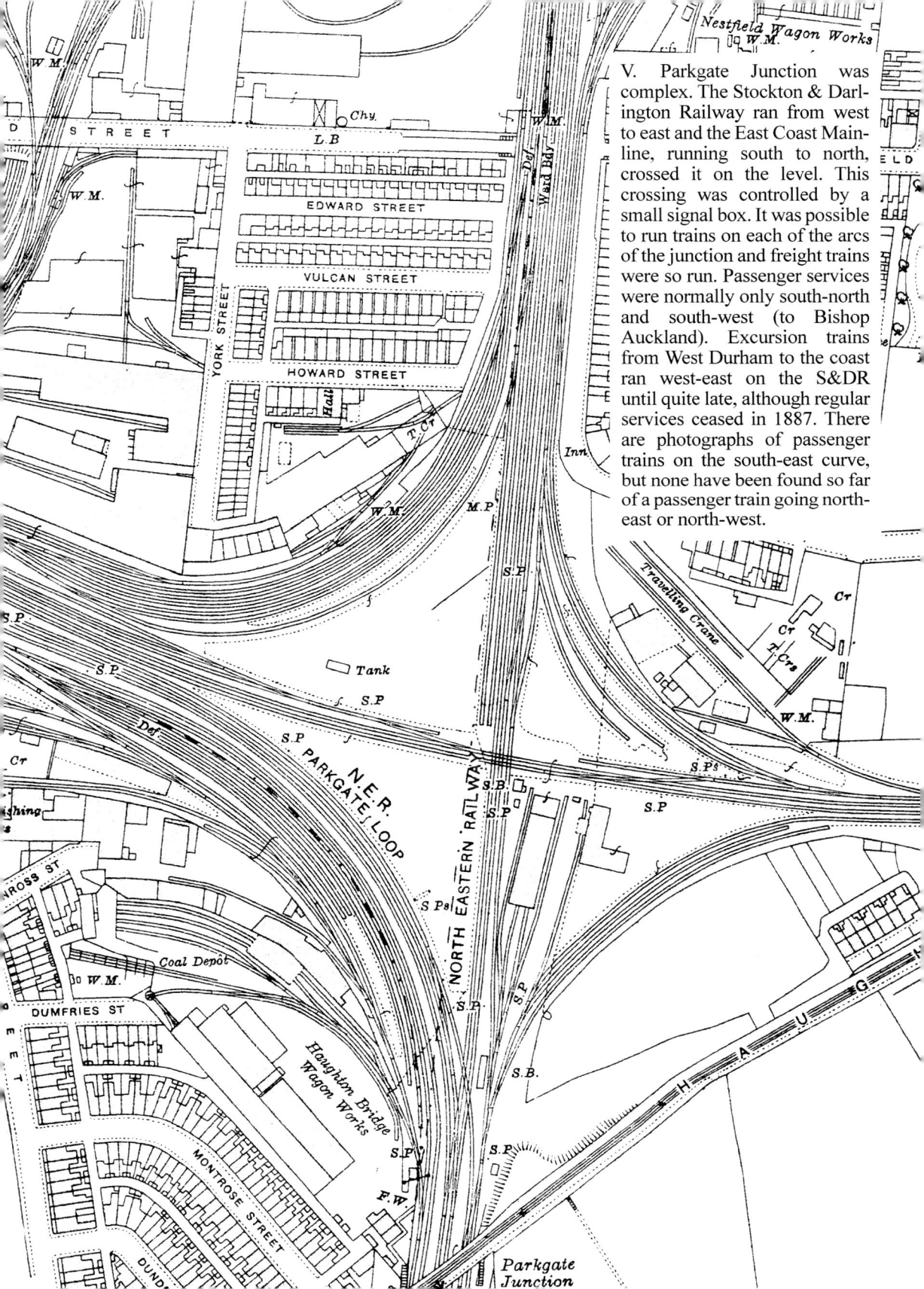

V. Parkgate Junction was complex. The Stockton & Darlington Railway ran from west to east and the East Coast Mainline, running south to north, crossed it on the level. This crossing was controlled by a small signal box. It was possible to run trains on each of the arcs of the junction and freight trains were so run. Passenger services were normally only south-north and south-west (to Bishop Auckland). Excursion trains from West Durham to the coast ran west-east on the S&DR until quite late, although regular services ceased in 1887. There are photographs of passenger trains on the south-east curve, but none have been found so far of a passenger train going north-east or north-west.

18. The LNER used the S&DR crossing for a publicity photograph which shows S&DR 0-4-0 *Locomotion No.1* superimposed on a photograph of class A1 (later A3) 4-6-2 no.2579 *Dick Turpin* just on the crossing with an up train to London. *Dick Turpin* became no.60080 and was a Newcastle engine from 1924 until May 1960. The crossing has gone, though the large engineering shed in the background still exists. There was an LNER cut out sign marking the crossing for passengers. It was still there in 2006, but lost in the line-side bushes. (LNER/K.Hoole coll.)

19. This shows the crossing viewed from Haughton Road bridge. Parkgate signal box covered the west to south junction. Behind Parkgate box is the GNofER engine shed of 1841. In 2006 this still existed though boarded up with no rail access. In 1954 class A8 4-6-2T no.69891 was hauling a diverted Darlington-Saltburn passenger train across the ECML on the S&D crossing which was controlled by the small signal box. (J.W.Armstrong Trust)

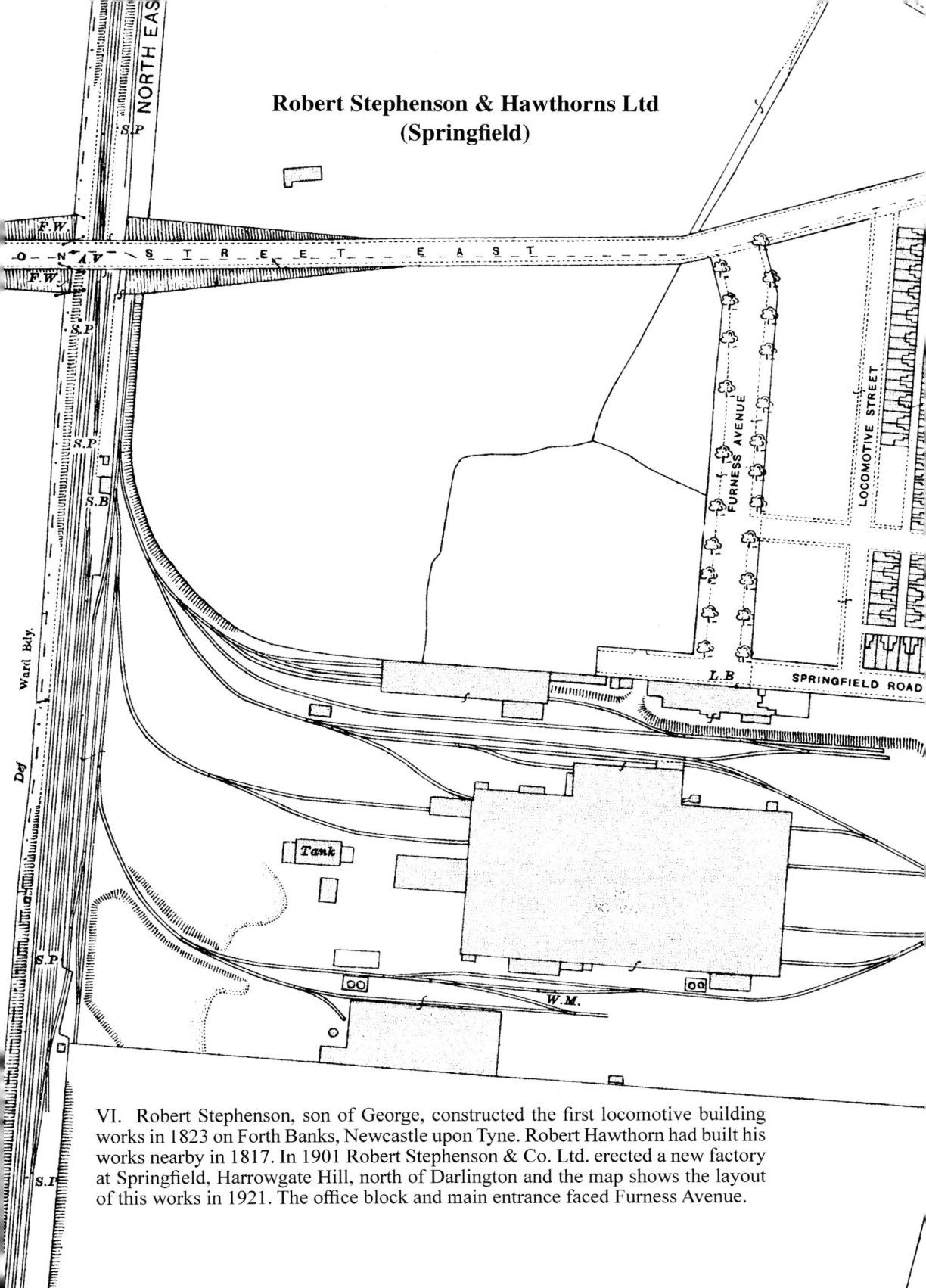

VI. Robert Stephenson, son of George, constructed the first locomotive building works in 1823 on Forth Banks, Newcastle upon Tyne. Robert Hawthorn had built his works nearby in 1817. In 1901 Robert Stephenson & Co. Ltd. erected a new factory at Springfield, Harrowgate Hill, north of Darlington and the map shows the layout of this works in 1921. The office block and main entrance faced Furness Avenue.

20. Springfield signal box was a favoured spot for North Eastern Railway historian and photographer, Jack Armstrong, mainly because it was at the end of his back garden. In this 1936 photograph class K3 2-6-0 no.75 (later no.61823) is unusually hauling a down express. Behind the signal box is the rail entrance to Robert Stephenson & Co. Ltd. which, in 1937, became Robert Stephenson & Hawthorns Ltd. (J.W.Armstrong Trust)

21. Robert Stephenson & Co. Ltd. opened the Springfield Works in 1902 and concentrated on building mainline steam locomotives here. This 1907 picture shows the offices at Springfield. The company became a subsidiary of the Vulcan Foundry from 1944 and part of English Electric in 1962. The Springfield Works closed on 1st May 1964. The site is now a landscaped park with new housing. (Darlington Library)

22. This is the erecting shop in 1927. The locomotives were from a batch of ten metre-gauge 4-6-0s for the South Indian Railway, including no.B122 which was Robert Stephenson & Hawthorns no.3939. The class B locomotives, RSH no.3931-3946, were a British Engineering Standards Association (BESA) passenger design. (Darlington Library)

AYCLIFFE

VII. Aycliffe station was convenient to the village. The River Skerne passed under the railway immediately to the north of the station platforms. The main buildings were on the down side with the signal box on the down platform. There was a 1½ ton crane in the goods siding. South of the station were the Aycliffe quarries. To the west was the Aycliffe Lime and Limestone Co. Ltd. and to the east, shown on the map, was the Ord & Maddison Ltd. quarry. Both quarries were rail served.

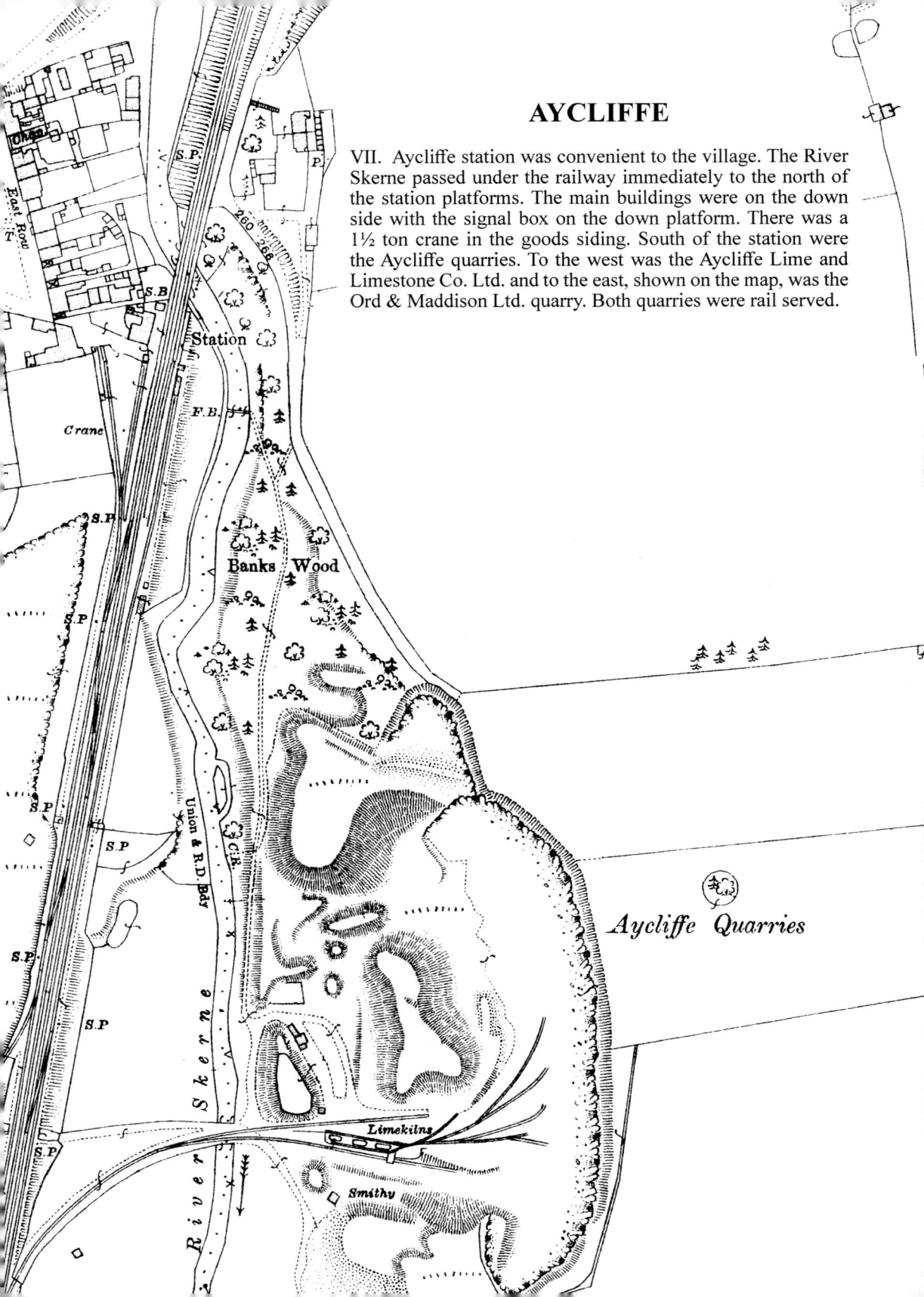

23. Class A1 4-6-2 no. 60126 *Sir Vincent Raven* is entering the station with the 6.52am Newcastle to York stopping train, departing Aycliffe 8.03am, on 28th February 1953. This was the last day of passenger service which formally closed on 2nd March. The stationmaster is present on this sad day. After closure the station was removed and the site is occupied by a modern office building with only a track access for permanent way staff. (J.W.Armstrong Trust)

24. The western quarry was started in the 1880s by George Hanson, a local farmer. Hanson, Brown & Co. Ltd worked it until 1920 with traffic shunted by NER locomotives. Aycliffe Lime & Limestone Co. Ltd. introduced their own locomotives from about 1923 and built this locomotive from a Foden steam lorry, works no. 8360. Photographed on 27th August 1948, it had been scrapped by January 1949. The firm became a subsidiary of Gjers, Mills & Co., Middlesbrough. Rail traffic was shunted by road tractor from 1961 and the quarry itself was closed shortly afterwards. (D.G.Charlton)

NORTH OF AYCLIFFE

25. The ECML passed underneath the Clarence Railway north of Aycliffe. The section of the CR from Shildon to Newport, Middlesbrough, was chosen by Sir Vincent Raven for his electrification trials. Here the bridge over the ECML was being renewed prior to the electrification which started 1st July 1915. We are looking south and only the road bridge now remains. (K.Hoole coll.)

26. While the electrified line with its ten Bo-BoWE freight locomotives satisfactorily hauled coal until 1934, Raven proposed to electrify the ECML. He built an experimental express passenger locomotive No.13, a 2-Co-2WE with 6ft. 8in. driving wheels. Here it is hauling a 16 coach test train and dynamometer car. The last coach is on the bridge over the ECML. Think what might have been if Raven's vision had resulted in an ECML electrified in 1923 instead of 1991. (K.Hoole coll.)

BRADBURY

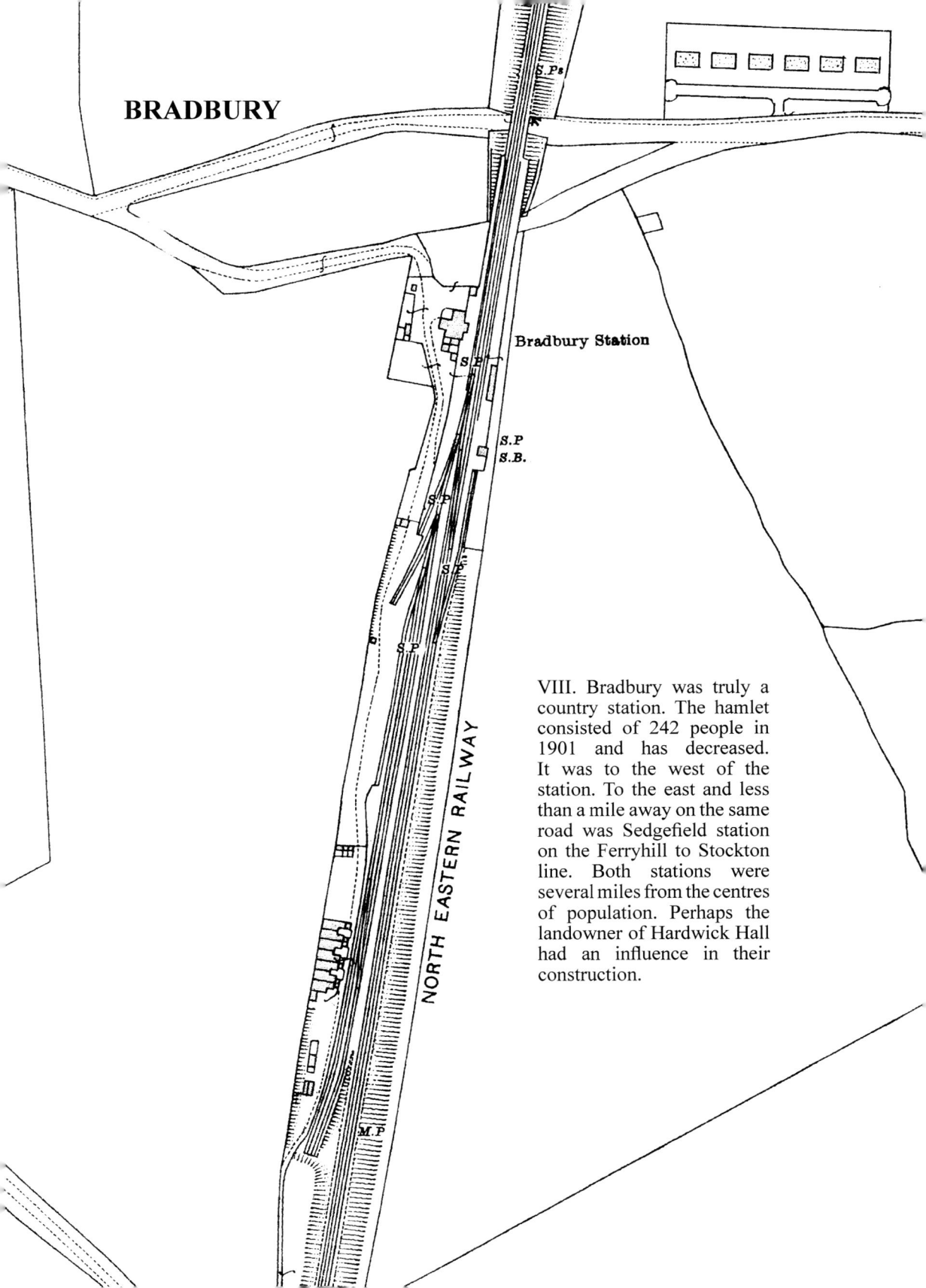

Bradbury Station

NORTH EASTERN RAILWAY

VIII. Bradbury was truly a country station. The hamlet consisted of 242 people in 1901 and has decreased. It was to the west of the station. To the east and less than a mile away on the same road was Sedgefield station on the Ferryhill to Stockton line. Both stations were several miles from the centres of population. Perhaps the landowner of Hardwick Hall had an influence in their construction.

27. We are looking north through the station. The trailing point leads to the goods yard, which, together with the station cottages and the main station buildings, were on the west side of the line. Behind the wooden signal gantry is the evidence of roof repairs to the stationmasters house. There is scaffolding on the other side of the building. The stationmaster is standing with his two children at the door to the up platform waiting room. (Beamish Museum)

28. The station was closed to passenger and goods traffic on 2nd January 1950. The wooden buildings had been removed by 1955 when 2MT 2-6-0 no.46474 entered the yard with a rail recovery train. The permanent way brake van is an old Great Northern four wheeled van. (Stations UK)

29. A more recent track-laying train passed through the site of the station on 13th February 2000. No. 66501 was a new loco when it hauled the Jarvis Rail Relaying system train from Tursdale to Doncaster. (P.J.Robinson)

NORTH OF BRADBURY

30. A branch line left the Stockton to Ferryhill route of the Clarence Railway at Chilton Bank Foot and crossed the ECML on its way to Chilton and Leasingthorne. This was always a freight only branch and it closed on 31st July 1961. The steam and banjo dome indicates a Pacific locomotive heading north on the ECML. The small community of derelict cottages rejoiced in the name of 'Linger and Die' and the overgrown nature of the branch reflected this on 24th August. (K.Hoole coll.)

FERRYHILL

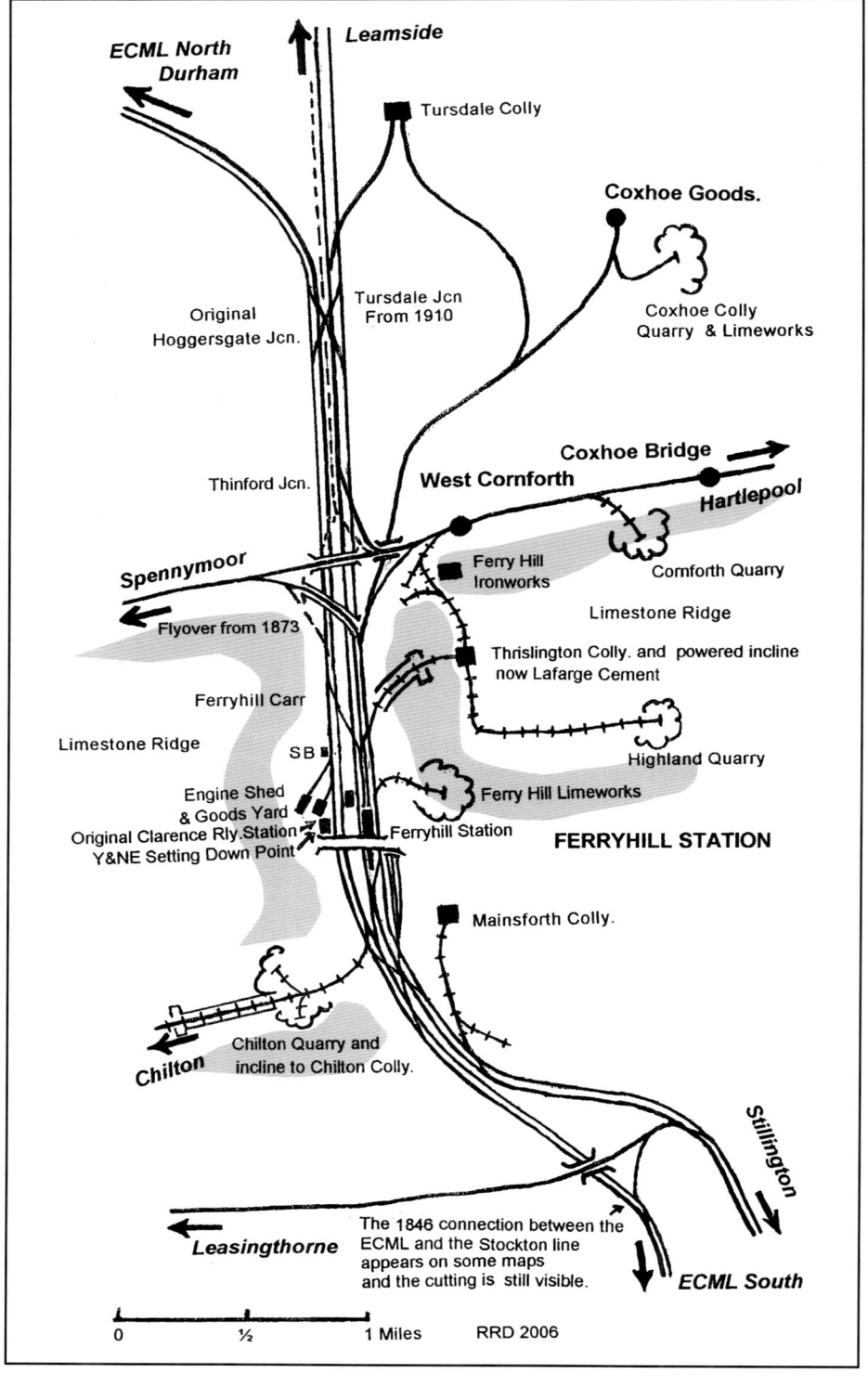

31. The Clarence Railway built a rather fine house at Ferryhill to be their station building. It later was the station masters house. By the 26th August 1966, subsidence had taken its toll and it was no longer habitable. It was demolished by July 1968. (K.Hoole coll.)

← IX. The Clarence Railway reached Ferryhill, first arriving from Stockton via Stillington. In 1835, they blasted and hewed a cutting 67ft deep and 75 yards wide through the limestone ridge, removing 100,000 cubic yards of material in the process. They aimed to reach the City of Durham but, exhausted by their efforts, went no further. However, over the following years a network of NER and industrial lines were built in the Ferryhill area and this sketch map gives their outline. The area was once market gardens for the Bishops of Durham. It was called Fergenc from 1256, Ferye-on-the-hill from 1316 and Ferryhill from 1648.

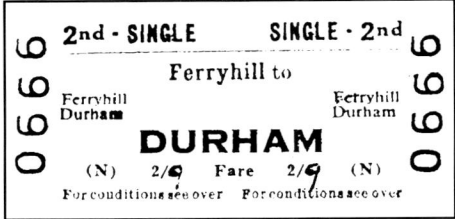

32. This indifferent postcard view of Ferryhill station shows the approach road to the NER station whose hipped glass platform roof can be seen on the left. Two coaches are visible in the south bay. Mainsforth Colliery remained in production until 3rd December 1968. The community of Ferryhill Station is distinct from Ferryhill which is on top of the hill. (Beamish Museum)

33. Ferryhill station, goods shed and engine shed are viewed from the western edge of the Ferryhill Gap. A class J21 0-6-0 is on shed. At least seventeen locomotives, including 0-6-0s, an 0-8-0 and a G5 0-4-4T, can be seen in the yard. In 1923 the shed allocation included two G5s, one J25, one J26 and nine J27s. In 1930 the last surviving McDonnell J22 0-6-0 was shedded here and in 1932 two Q5 0-8-0s arrived. The shed was closed in November 1938 and the building was finally demolished in 1954. The goods shed still remains, though in private use, and the 3-ton crane has long gone. (K.Hoole coll.)

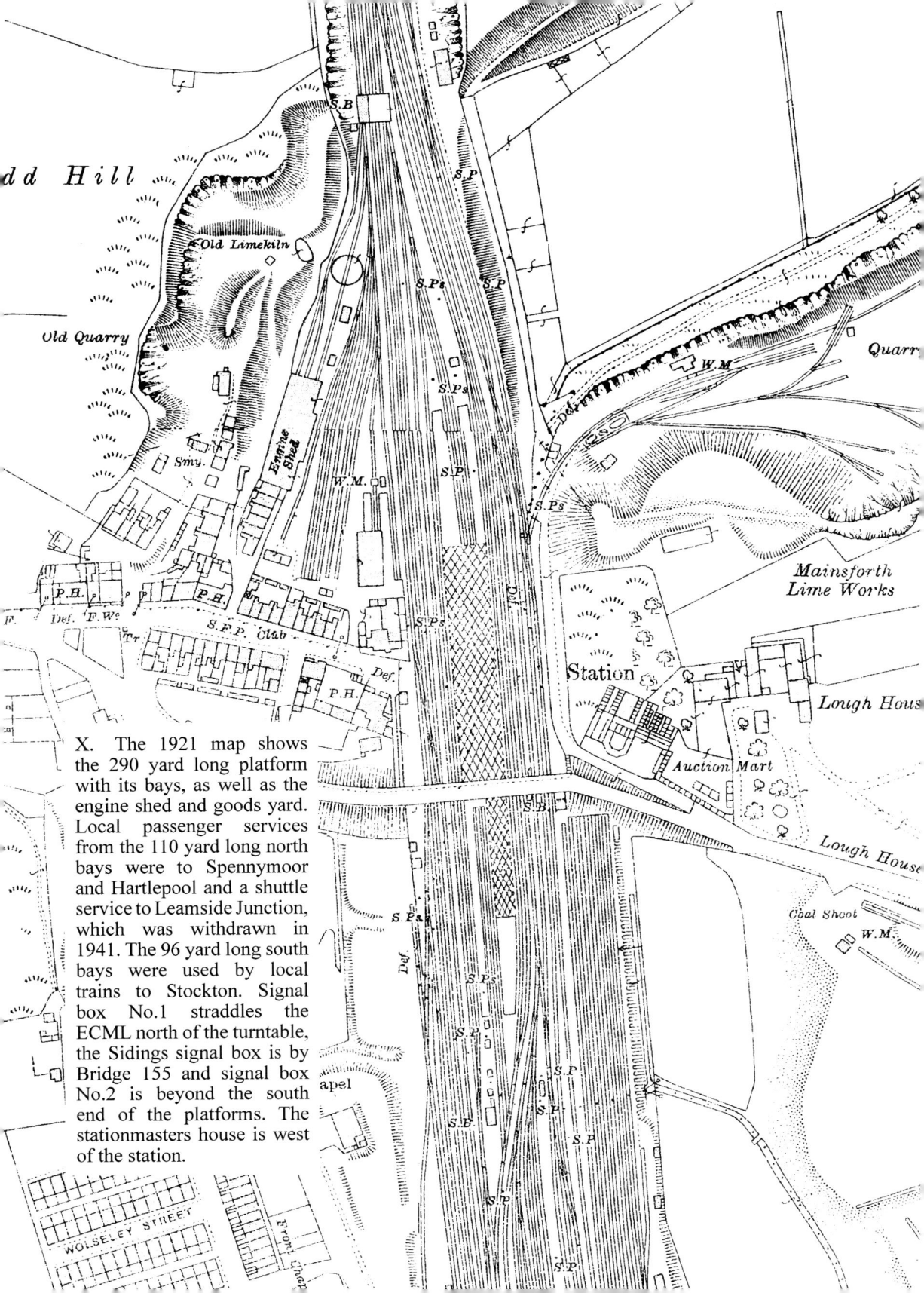

X. The 1921 map shows the 290 yard long platform with its bays, as well as the engine shed and goods yard. Local passenger services from the 110 yard long north bays were to Spennymoor and Hartlepool and a shuttle service to Leamside Junction, which was withdrawn in 1941. The 96 yard long south bays were used by local trains to Stockton. Signal box No.1 straddles the ECML north of the turntable, the Sidings signal box is by Bridge 155 and signal box No.2 is beyond the south end of the platforms. The stationmasters house is west of the station.

34. The population of Ferryhill increased threefold to over 10,500 by 1961 and by 1955 the station awning had been modernised, though the platforms were still gas lit. Spennymoor and Hartlepool services from the northern bays were withdrawn in 1952. The ECML through lines are to the right. Ferryhill enjoyed mainline status into the 1960s with at least six stopping trains in each direction on weekdays and more on Saturdays. (Stations UK)

35. Besides the gaslights, there are three NER snake seats on platform 1, though only the centre one has complete snake tails. The three lads are watching the progress of WD 2-8-0 no.90465, a Newport 51B shed locomotive, as it rumbles past with a class H express freight. (Stations UK)

36. Our photographer is a passenger in a northbound DMU and his train has been given the road ahead from Ferryhill No.1 signal box. The station closed to passengers on 6th March 1967. Local people feel that this was for operating convenience rather than lack of passengers.
(J.W.Armstrong Trust)

37. The station site had been cleared by 26th September 1980, when Deltic no. 55022 *Royal Scots Grey* was heading north with the 7.22am Plymouth to Edinburgh train. There was some residual activity in the goods yard, with a once-daily goods pick-up from Teesside. The decline in coal production and the movement of goods traffic to the roads, saw the closure of Ferryhill's goods and mineral yards, both down and up. However, the remaining sidings are used by block freight trains.
(T.Heavyside)

38. Ferryhill had at least six signal boxes. The Sidings box, south of the station roadbridge closed in 1954. No.1 and Coxhoe Junction boxes were elevated NER boxes that straddled the running lines and No.2 and Tursdale were more conventional lineside buildings. No.2 was rebuilt and reopened on 13th December 1953. It is still open to deal with activities on the Tursdale Junction to Stockton line, having lost its ECML responsibilities with the opening of the Tyneside Integrated Electronic Control Centre (IECC) at Chaytor's Bank, Gateshead. An up GNER express is passing on the ECML on 22nd August 2006, propelled by no. 91104 *Grantham*. (R.R.Darsley)

NORTH OF FERRYHILL

39. Looking north from the station site, we can see the wooded cliff that is the Clarence Railway cutting. A BR permanent way crew van is parked behind the goods shed. No. 40026 is on the up Leamside line and will head south with a parcels train on 3rd September 1977. The white building on the crest of the cutting is a pigeon cree and pigeon specials coming from Ashington, Morpeth and Tyneside also collected at Ferryhill on their way south to Huntingdon and Hitchin. (T.Heavyside)

40. In the distance is the east face of the Ferryhill Gap. On the ridge is the very large LaFarge cement works and below it in the trees are the silos of the rail loading terminal. This is the remaining source of freight traffic from Ferryhill and no. 60041 has just collected a rake of lime containers for Margam (South Wales) and is heading for the junction of the siding with the Tursdale Junction to Stockton Line. A signalman from Ferryhill No.2 is following in his car having locked the ground frame controlling the sidings to the silos. The date is 21st September 2006. (R.R.Darsley)

41. Coxhoe Junction signal box (55 levers) was over the Tursdale Junction to Stockton line and controlled access to the Coxhoe Goods branch and the line to West Cornforth and Hartlepool. The tall signal on the up fast mainline was known locally as Big Bertha. A class Q6 0-8-0 is hauling its train of empty coal hoppers for the Dean and Chapter colliery onto the flyover towards Spennymoor. Before this bridge was built, the line to Spennymoor diverged to the right on the low embankment. This involved goods trains crossing the ECML to get to the yards. The siding in the foreground led back through the Gap to the goods and engine sheds. (N.E.Stead coll.)

42. At Tursdale Junction, the present ECML diverges from the original route north, the Leamside line. On 22nd August 2006 no. 66016 with a train of EWS coal hoppers is crossing to the ECML to continue north. The Leamside line has been reduced to a single track and mothballed, though if restored, it could still provide relief capacity to the ECML, as it used to do. (R.R.Darsley)

43. On the broad sweeping curve from Tursdale to Croxdale there is a deep cutting. Hett Steps was a public footpath across the ECML in this cutting. On 23rd April 1990, it was protected by a 'train on way' signal, though later telephones were installed. In October 1994 a footpath diversion order was made to a new footbridge over the railway. (I.S.Carr)

CROXDALE

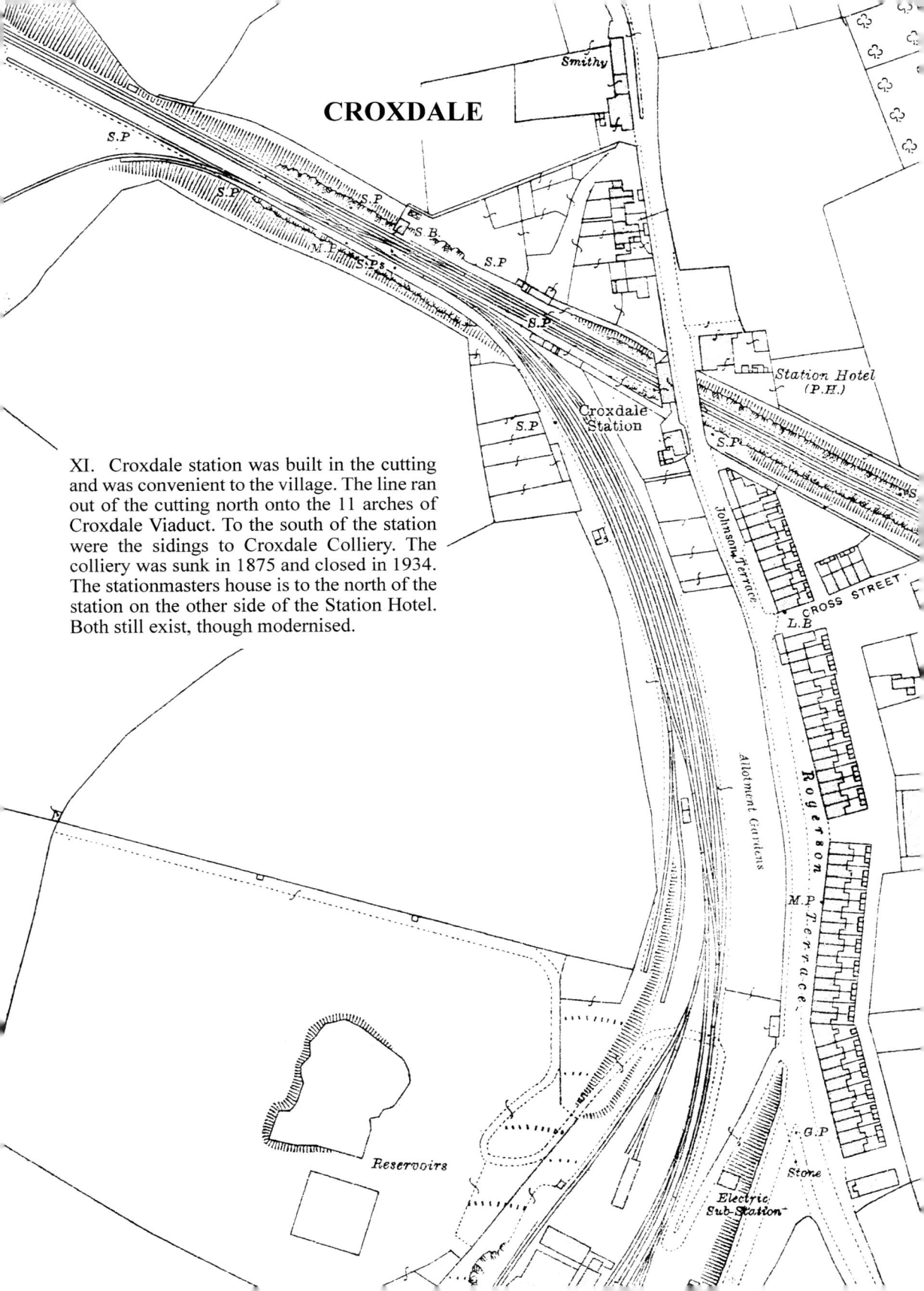

XI. Croxdale station was built in the cutting and was convenient to the village. The line ran out of the cutting north onto the 11 arches of Croxdale Viaduct. To the south of the station were the sidings to Croxdale Colliery. The colliery was sunk in 1875 and closed in 1934. The stationmasters house is to the north of the station on the other side of the Station Hotel. Both still exist, though modernised.

44. We are looking south at the buildings of Croxdale station in the 1930s. The main ticket office with the station clock is on the overbridge. Through that bridge, part of the arch of Sunderland Bridge can be seen. While it could not be described as a pretty station, the roses and flowerbeds brought colour to the scene. The station closed to passenger and goods traffic on 26th September 1938. (Stations UK)

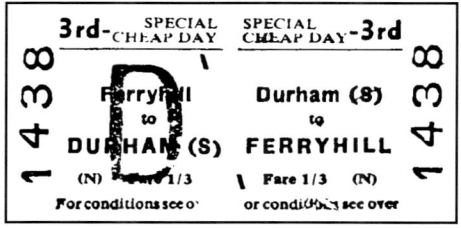 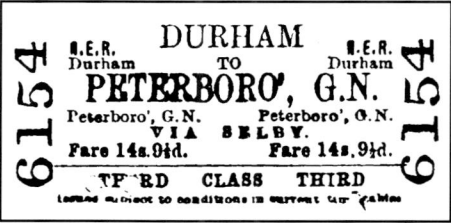

45. Croxdale Viaduct (198 yards long) is immediately north of the station and spans the River Wear with nine brick arches. Class D49 4-4-0 no.365 *The Morpeth* (later no. 62768) is going south on 16th February 1939 with a train composed of East Coast Joint Stock carriages and Great Western Railway carriages. This was probably the 'Port to Port' express from Newcastle to Swansea. In 2006, the growth of trees along the river and the construction of a small sewage farm have restricted the view, but it is still possible to observe the grandeur of the construction. (LNER/K.Hoole coll.)

46. The Langley Moor viaduct is different in style with 132 yards of metal lattice work between the six straight brick pillars. The original viaduct was wooden. Class K3 2-6-0 no. 61952 crosses with an up freight on 7th June 1952. (J.W.Armstrong Trust)

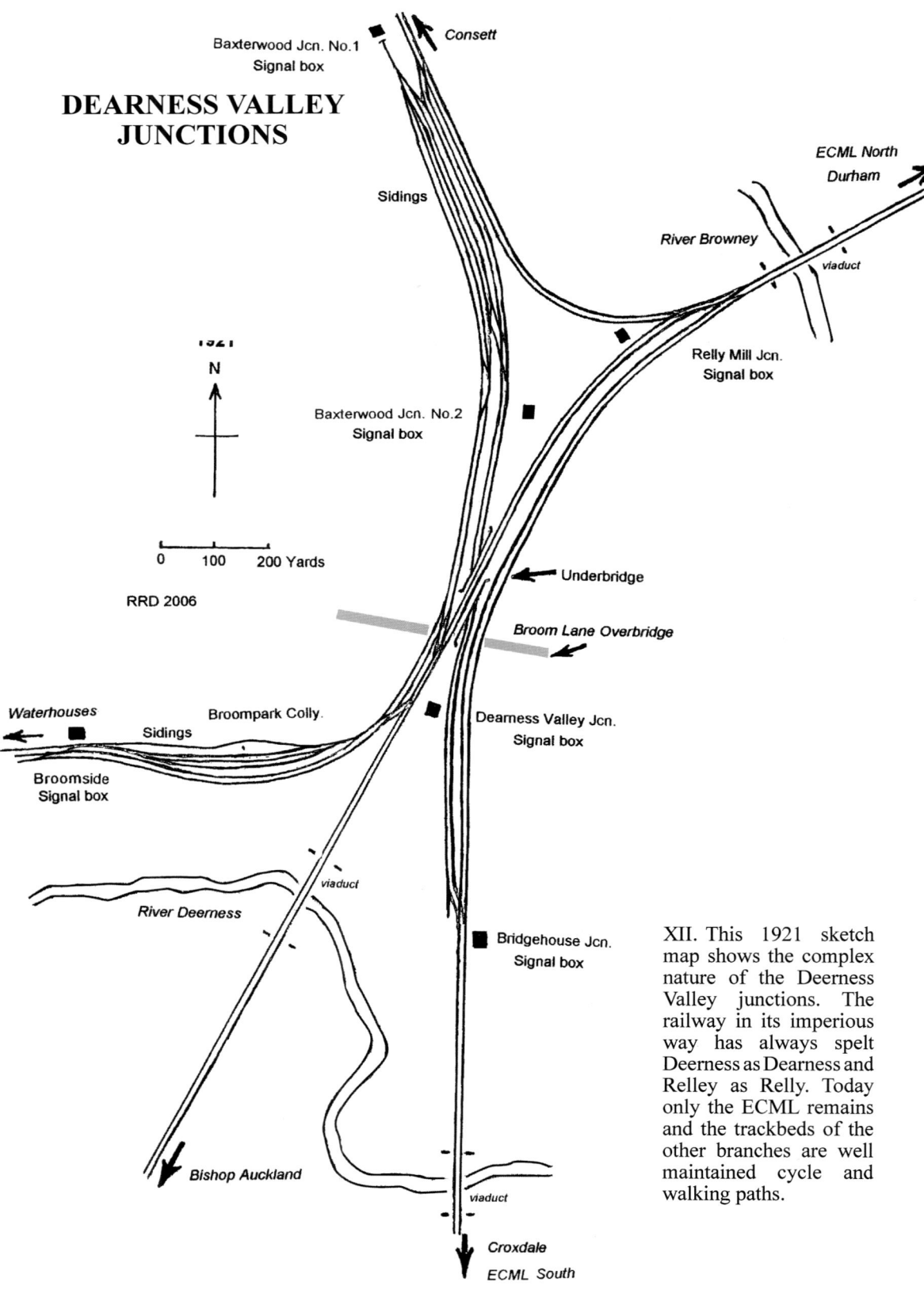

XII. This 1921 sketch map shows the complex nature of the Deerness Valley junctions. The railway in its imperious way has always spelt Deerness as Dearness and Relley as Relly. Today only the ECML remains and the trackbeds of the other branches are well maintained cycle and walking paths.

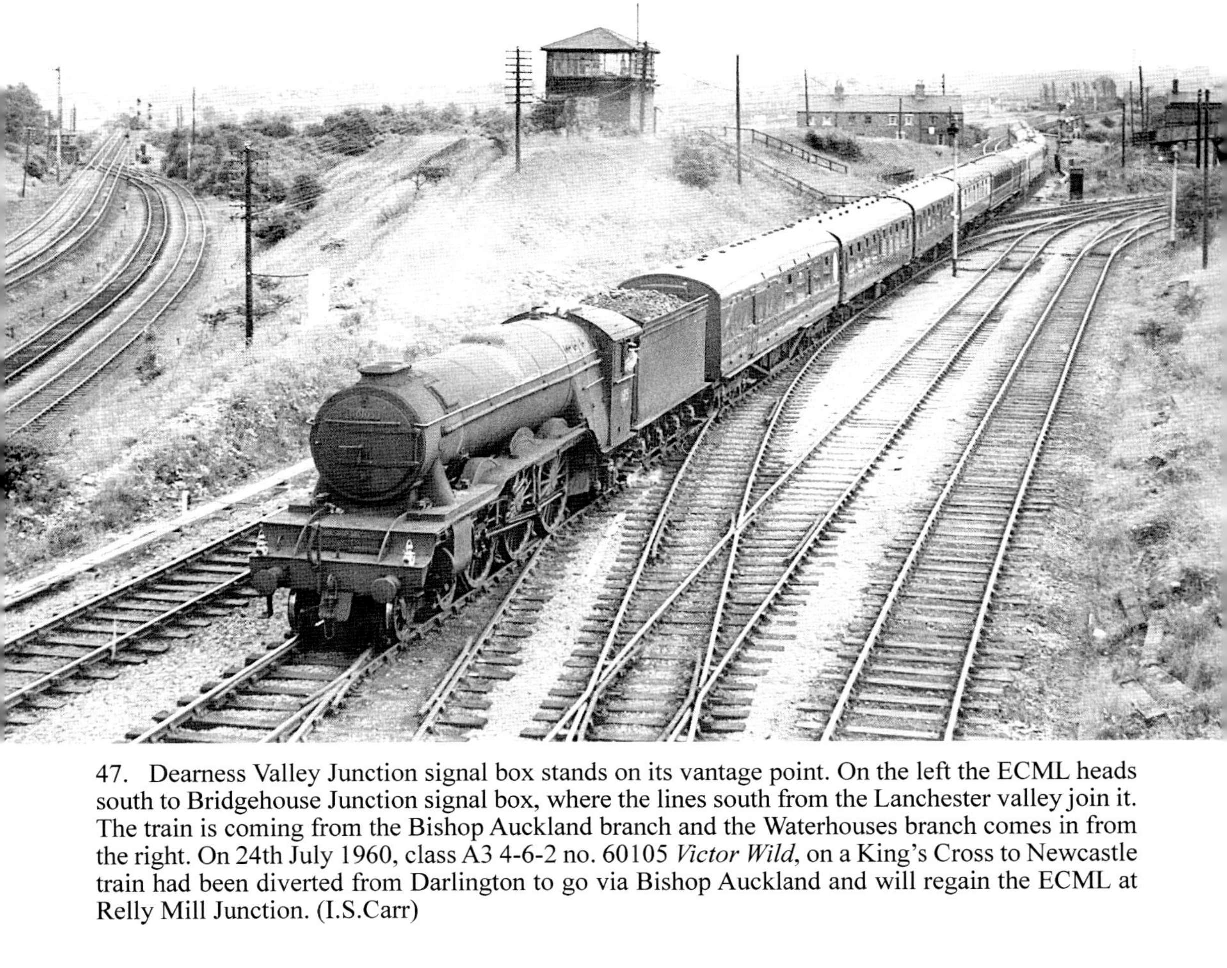

47. Dearness Valley Junction signal box stands on its vantage point. On the left the ECML heads south to Bridgehouse Junction signal box, where the lines south from the Lanchester valley join it. The train is coming from the Bishop Auckland branch and the Waterhouses branch comes in from the right. On 24th July 1960, class A3 4-6-2 no. 60105 *Victor Wild*, on a King's Cross to Newcastle train had been diverted from Darlington to go via Bishop Auckland and will regain the ECML at Relly Mill Junction. (I.S.Carr)

0497 L. N. E. R. PRIVILEGE 0497
FOR CONDITIONS SEE BACK
PLAWSWORTH to
CHESTER-LE-STREET
Available within one week of date of issue.
THIRD / S. P. 3413 CHESTER-LE-ST \ CLASS

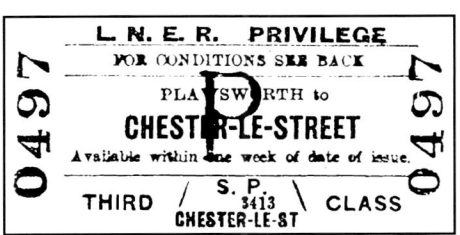

48. With the closure of the branch lines, the opportunity was taken in November 1974 to re-align the ECML onto the trackbed of the lines from Lanchester Valley to ease the curve on the main line. The site of Bridgehouse Junction signal box is opposite the rear of this GNER High Speed Train. Powered by no. 43118 *City of Kingston upon Hull* and no. 43080, it was approaching the Broom Lane overbridge on 6th July 2006. (R.R.Darsley)

49. Class Q6 0-8-0 no.63448 has brought a load of steel products from Consett Steelworks down the Lanchester Valley and is waiting access to the Bishop Auckland line. Type 4 no. D240 with an up ECML express has been diverted via Bishop Auckland and has left the main line at Relly Mill Junction whose signal box is visible in the distance. The ECML can be seen dipping down to the right. In the background is Relly Mill Viaduct. Passing under the girder bridge is the connection to the ECML from Lanchester. The chalk graffiti on the Wickham rail trolley shed by the water crane is more artistic than most. The date is 17th July 1960. (I.S.Carr)

50. The previous views were taken from the Broom Lane overbridge (B6302). This pleasant stone viaduct became insufficient for modern road traffic and was replaced in 2005 by a metal and concrete structure just to the south. In a tribute to the popularity of the old bridge as a place to watch trains, its western abutment has been made into an official view site. This clever piece of iron work depicting a class 47 diesel arriving with its train at a station is the back rest of the viewing seat. (R.R.Darsley)

51. The northern end of the complex junction was controlled by Relly Mill signal box and the 12.07pm Darlington-Bishop Auckland-Newcastle train, hauled by B1 class 4-6-0 no.61032, *Stembok*, has regained the ECML and is crossing Relly Mill viaduct. The viaduct has six arches and is 400ft long and 65ft high. Since this date, Saturday 23rd July 1960, tree growth on both sides of the viaduct mean that it can no longer be photographed in this way. (I.S.Carr)

52. After Relly Mill viaduct the ECML runs into Redhills cutting, down the bank, across Durham viaduct and into North Road station. A feature on the down line on this bank was an automatic mail exchange point. In this photograph class A1 4-6-2 no. 60115 *Meg Merrilies* is almost level with the operator's hut and the mail bag catching net. The headcode indicates that *Meg Merrilies* was hauling a through freight on 16th June 1962. (R.R.Darsley)

53. Coming up the 1 in 101 bank with a southbound train was an effort, especially if the locomotive had a standing start from Durham station in wet weather. Despite the large black thundercloud class A1 4-6-2 no. 60126 *Sir Vincent Raven* is making light work of the climb on 16th June 1962. (R.R.Darsley)

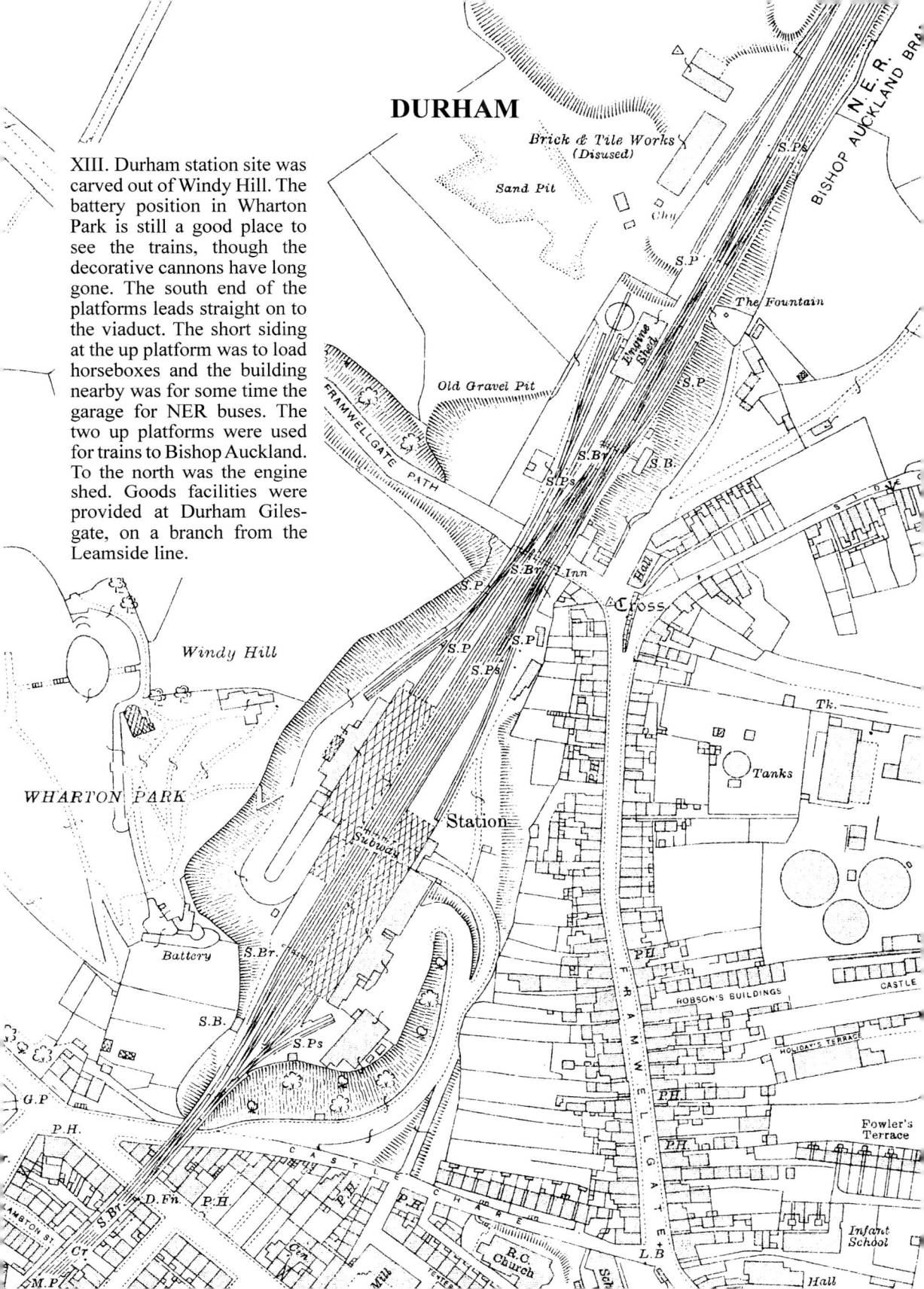

DURHAM

XIII. Durham station site was carved out of Windy Hill. The battery position in Wharton Park is still a good place to see the trains, though the decorative cannons have long gone. The south end of the platforms leads straight on to the viaduct. The short siding at the up platform was to load horseboxes and the building nearby was for some time the garage for NER buses. The two up platforms were used for trains to Bishop Auckland. To the north was the engine shed. Goods facilities were provided at Durham Gilesgate, on a branch from the Leamside line.

54. Durham Viaduct was not built for the grand trunk railway to Scotland. It was built by the Sunderland & Bishop Auckland Railway promoted by people who wanted to divert some of West Durham's coal from the Tees to the Wear. There was more money in moving coal than people. The viaduct, seen under construction, was opened in 1857. Durham Castle is visible through the wooden formers for the arches. The wooden tower appears to be moveable from arch to arch and gives some idea of the final height. (K.Hoole coll.)

55. Designed by T.E.Harrison, the curved viaduct of 11 arches is 100ft high and 704 yards long. Its tapered piers sit on coped plinths and are of rock faced sandstone with ashlars dressing. The imposing signal gantry has long gone, but when the ECML was electrified, specially designed catenary was used to minimise the effect on the view of the viaduct. On Saturday 19th August 1961, 4MT 2-6-0 no.43126 drifts into Durham with the 11.20am Blackpool Central to Newcastle via Tebay, Stainmore and Bishop Auckland. (I.S.Carr)

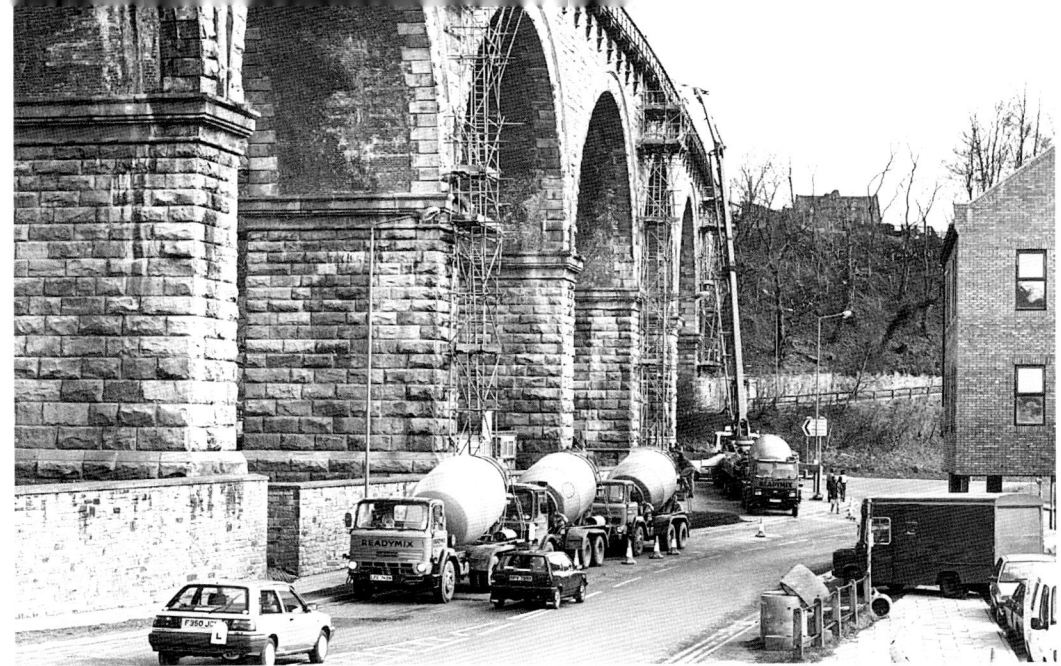

56. In preparation for the ECML electrification, repairs and modifications were made to the viaduct. On 13th March 1989, concrete is being pumped to the top of the structure to make a new track bed. Scaffolding is to allow the construction of bases for the electrification masts. A plaque in Durham station commemorated the erection of the 200,000th mast in the electrification of the ECML. (I.S.Carr)

57. By standing at the south end of the up platform it was possible to photograph trains coming off the viaduct. A very good day for this was Miners' Gala Day, when there were many special workings to bring miners' families from all over the county to Durham for parades, politics and picnics on the race course. On Gala Day 20th July 1963, class B1 4-6-0 no. 61019 *Nilghai* brings empty stock from the Dearness Valley Junctions sidings to form the 8.17am train for Sunderland. (I.S.Carr)

58. The panorama of Durham Cathedral and Durham Castle from the railway is one of the most spectacular views in northern Europe. In the 1930s, it was the LNER custom to marshal their coaches on prestige trains with the corridors to the west. This gave the best views of Durham and the Northumbrian coast to passengers seated in the compartments. (R.R.Darsley)

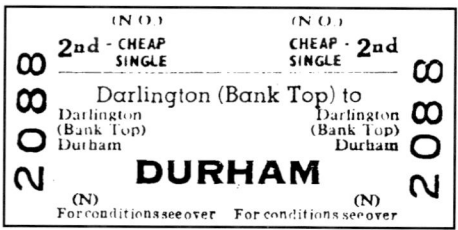

59. Not so frequently seen is the view of the railway from the top of the tower of Durham Cathedral. The viaduct strides across the city and the station is on a shelf above the Roman Catholic church. North Road climbs towards the horizon and the new University Hospital. To the right is County Hall, the home of Durham County Council and Record Office. (R.R.Darsley)

60. The main entrance to the station faced over the city. The bunting and banners were to celebrate the coronation of Queen Elizabeth II on 2nd June 1953. The steep road up to the station continued underneath the platforms to the buildings on the down platform. (K.Hoole coll.)

61. Banking locomotives were used at Durham in steam days for any up stopping train over 11 coaches long. The banker was usually a G5 0-4-4T, A8 4-6-2T, V1 or V3 2-6-2T. Here G5 no.67298 is pushing hard to get the evening mail out of the station. Banking locomotives were withdrawn in 1964 and thereafter locomotives had to manage on their own. (J.W.Armstrong Trust)

62. Serious deterioration of the canopy and some of the buildings on the up side led to modernisation in the 1970s that was a complete mismatch of architectural styles. This shows the staircase and road tunnel leading from the upside buildings to the downside. It had not weathered well by 2006. (R.R.Darsley)

63. The downside buildings and platforms were the original station and restoration of the canopy was being carried out more sympathetically in 2006. It has always been a stiff uphill walk from the city centre to the station, but the Durham Cathedral Bus has connected the station, bus station, market place and cathedral every twenty minutes in daytime since 2002. (R.R.Darsley)

64. The station can be exposed to northern weather. This is 6th March 1998 and the snow is lying as no. 91005 propels the 6.15am Kings Cross to Edinburgh into the station. Both train and engine appear reversed as the locomotive normally leads from Kings Cross and then the 'blunt end' is not normally visible. (I.S.Carr)

65. The arrival of no. 220016 *Midland Voyager* on the 13.32 Newcastle to Bristol working on 20th June 2006 allows comparison of the 1970s replacement canopy and the restored NER canopy. The two down bay platforms used for trains to Sunderland or Newcastle have been converted into extra car parking spaces and the up platform has been lengthened. (R.R.Darsley)

NORTH OF DURHAM

66. North of the platforms was the Durham North signal box (115 levers) and the engine shed. A NER up express hauled by T.W.Worsdell's J class, 4-2-2 no.1521 is approaching Durham. The J class locos, with 7ft 7in driving wheels, were the NER equivalent of GNR no.1 and the Midland singles. Originally compounds, they were highly successful as two cylinder simples and took quite a big share in the 1895 Race to Aberdeen. (K.Hoole coll.)

67. This is a clearer view of the two road single ended locomotive shed in BR days when it was a sub-shed of Sunderland South Dock. A very grimy class G5, 0-4-4T no. 67248, is standing over the inspection pit. The G5 tanks were finally displaced by diesel multiple units and 67248 was one of the last to be withdrawn, in December 1958. The shed itself was closed and demolished in 1961 to provide space for an extended goods yard and the closure of Durham (Gilesgate). (A.R.Thompson coll.)

68. Newton Hall junction was where the ECML diverged from the Sunderland line. The Sunderland line swung to the right as it left the cutting and the ECML to the left. When the Sunderland line closed, the junction was swept away and the ECML realigned in April 1970 to ease the curve. On 21st August 1961, class A2 4-6-2 no. 60526 *Sugar Palm* is crossing the junction with the up "Norseman". This train from Tyne Commission Quay to Kings Cross connected with Scandinavian ferryboats. (I.S.Carr)

69. One and a half miles north of Newton Hall Junction and just south of Plawsworth was a NER branch to Kimblesworth Colliery. A mile long and mainly in cuttings, it was rarely photographed. It crossed the A1 (now A167) by a three arched viaduct, pictured here. This was a local landmark and fortunately had room for the second carriageway when the A1 was widened. The colliery closed on 4th November 1967 and the viaduct was demolished when further road improvements were made. (K.Hoole coll.)

70. Immediately north of the Kimblesworth Junction is the six-arch 132 yd. Plawsworth Viaduct. The junction can just be seen behind the end of the train which is a special from Peterborough to Newcastle hauled by class A3 4-6-2 no.4472 *Flying Scotsman*. The locomotive has its second tender, converted to a water carrier, in tow. The date is 10th September 1967 and since then the tree growth is such that it is impossible to photograph the viaduct from either side. (J.M.Boyes)

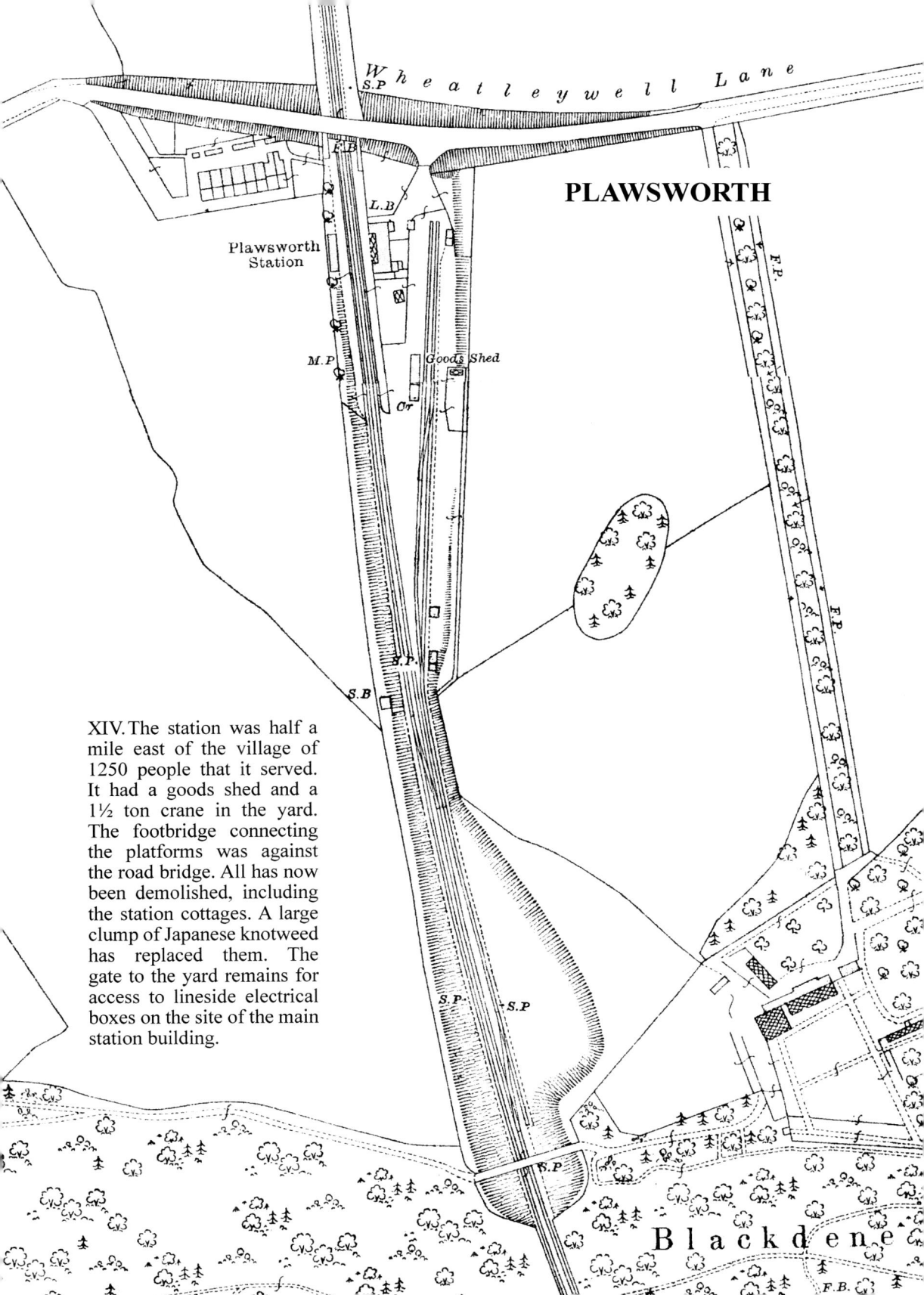

PLAWSWORTH

XIV. The station was half a mile east of the village of 1250 people that it served. It had a goods shed and a 1½ ton crane in the yard. The footbridge connecting the platforms was against the road bridge. All has now been demolished, including the station cottages. A large clump of Japanese knotweed has replaced them. The gate to the yard remains for access to lineside electrical boxes on the site of the main station building.

71. This is the station about 1912. The substantial brick building has its determined symmetry spoilt by the extra chimney. The floral displays are built up with pot plants. Advertisements for Walter Willson's, the local grocery chain, and for Empire Publications can be deciphered. A standard NER wooden waiting room was on the up platform. (Lens of Sutton coll.)

72. The station closed on 7th April 1952, but the station house was still occupied in 1959 with flowers growing along the railings. The platforms had recently been cleared away giving more room for class V2 2-6-2 no. 60934 to storm south with a through freight. (Stations UK)

73. Class A1 4-6-2 no. 60153 *Flamboyant* was working the 10.05 am York to Newcastle train past Plawsworth signal box into the station on 6th June 1960. The signals indicate an up train is also due. The siding to the goods yard was in use until 30th September 1963. (H.B.Priestley coll.)

CHESTER MOOR VIADUCT

74. A mile to the north is Chester Moor Viaduct over the South Burn tributary of the River Wear. Class A2 4-6-2 no. 60539 *Bronzino* is hauling a down express passenger train over the six-arch viaduct. The trees now crowd in so closely that the viaduct cannot be seen. In fact, in 2006 several small trees were growing *from* the viaduct. (J.W.Armstrong Trust)

75. Chester-le-Street is the major town between Durham and the outer suburbs of Newcastle. Between 1901 and 1961, it doubled in size to 20,000 people. This view in 1912 is to the north and a NER V class 4-4-2, possibly no.1776, is entering the station, while a freight engine is in the goods siding. A wicker laundry basket is on the trolley and the gardening is helped by the heated greenhouse on the side of the station. (Lens of Sutton coll.)

76. At the north end of the platforms was the signal box and a large water tank. The shadow of the goods shed is behind the public warning sign. NER class R 4-4-0 no.1078 (later D20 no. 62383) hurries south with a through van train. (K.Hoole coll.)

77. By 1970 the station was an unmanned halt. The goods yards closed on 4th October 1965, but the goods shed is still in use by a woodworking firm. The boarded up station building has seen a revival since, thanks to 'Chester-le-Track', a travel agent actively promoting rail travel. Alex Nelson is the proprietor and self-styled 'stationmaster'. (Lens of Sutton coll.)

78. This view of the roadside of the station in August 2006 shows that, although the chimneys have been capped and some windows blocked up, the buildings are very much as built. In 2006 it housed the travel agency, a café, a printer and a taxi firm. Space is still to let and the car park is full of commuters' cars. (R.R.Darsley)

79. There has been a revival in passenger services and Virgin Trains use the station as well as the First Trans-Pennine and Northern franchises. With electrification, the platforms have been upgraded and a new waiting shelter built on the down platform. Class 185 DMUs entered service on 28th August 2006. Here no.185112 stops on a Manchester Airport to Newcastle run on 21st September 2006. (R.R.Darsley)

80. Just north of the station is yet another fine viaduct. The 11-arched viaduct is 750ft long and 90ft high. The arches are semi-elliptical of 60ft span; the style is light red engineering brick in English Bond on stone plinths. It has a curve of one mile radius. The date is 29th August 1974 as nos. 37164 and 37163 cross with a Redcar-Consett iron ore train of 100 ton tippler wagons. (T.Heavyside)

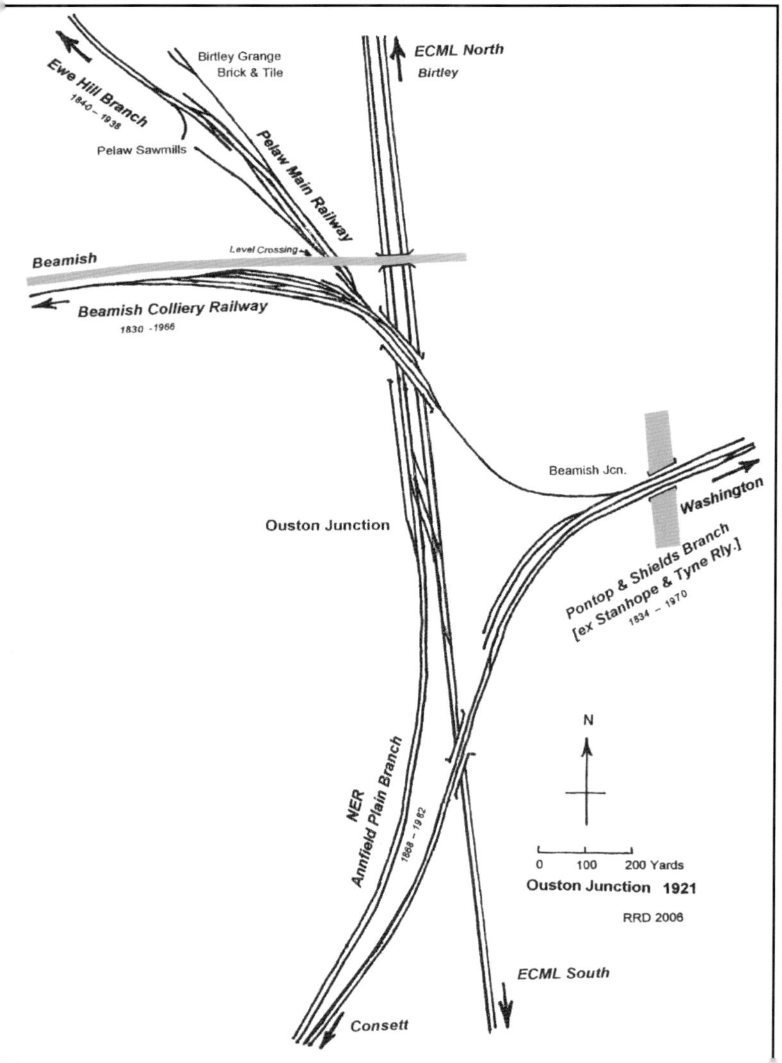

81. Super Voyager no. 221101 *Louis Blériot* heads south across the viaduct under the electrification catenary on 22nd August 2006. The workshops under the viaduct have been cleared and replaced by a Tesco supermarket car park, but it is still a good photographic opportunity. (R.R.Darsley)

OUSTON JUNCTION

XVI. This was another of County Durham's complicated interchanges between mainline railways and the private coal railways and waggonways that, in 1947, were vested in the National Coal Board. In 1921 the ECML was crossed by the NER Pontop and South Shields branch. The private Beamish waggonway also crossed the ECML by a broad bridge on which were storage sidings, reflecting that the waggonway had been built first. Joining the Beamish waggonway was the Ewe Hill branch of Pelaw Main Railway.

82. The photographer was standing on the Pontop and South Shields branch overbridge as he captured class A1 4-6-2 no. 60129 *Guy Mannering* heading south with a rather motley collection of stock. Behind the train is the flat roof of Ouston Junction signal box. A row of NCB 20-ton hopper wagons were in the Beamish waggonway sidings and the Ouston Colliery pit heaps were behind them. The date was 4th December 1953. (J.W.Armstrong Trust)

83. The photograph of no. 254.009 on a crew training trip was taken on 5th April, 1978 from the Beamish waggonway embankment. Behind the third coach are the lines connecting to the Pontop and South Shields branch. This was famous for the Tyne Dock to Consett ore trains. (I.S.Carr)

BIRTLEY

XVII. The NER quadrupled the track between Ouston and Low Fell in the early 1900s and Birtley station shows the effect of that. The station was surrounded by the clay pits for brickworks and these had narrow gauge railways to the clay face. The successors to the Union Brickworks and the tinplate works still occupy their sites, but to the south east the brickworks site has been redeveloped. The station, the hotel and the station cottages have been cleared away. The goods yard with its 5-ton crane has been replaced by a secure storage firm.

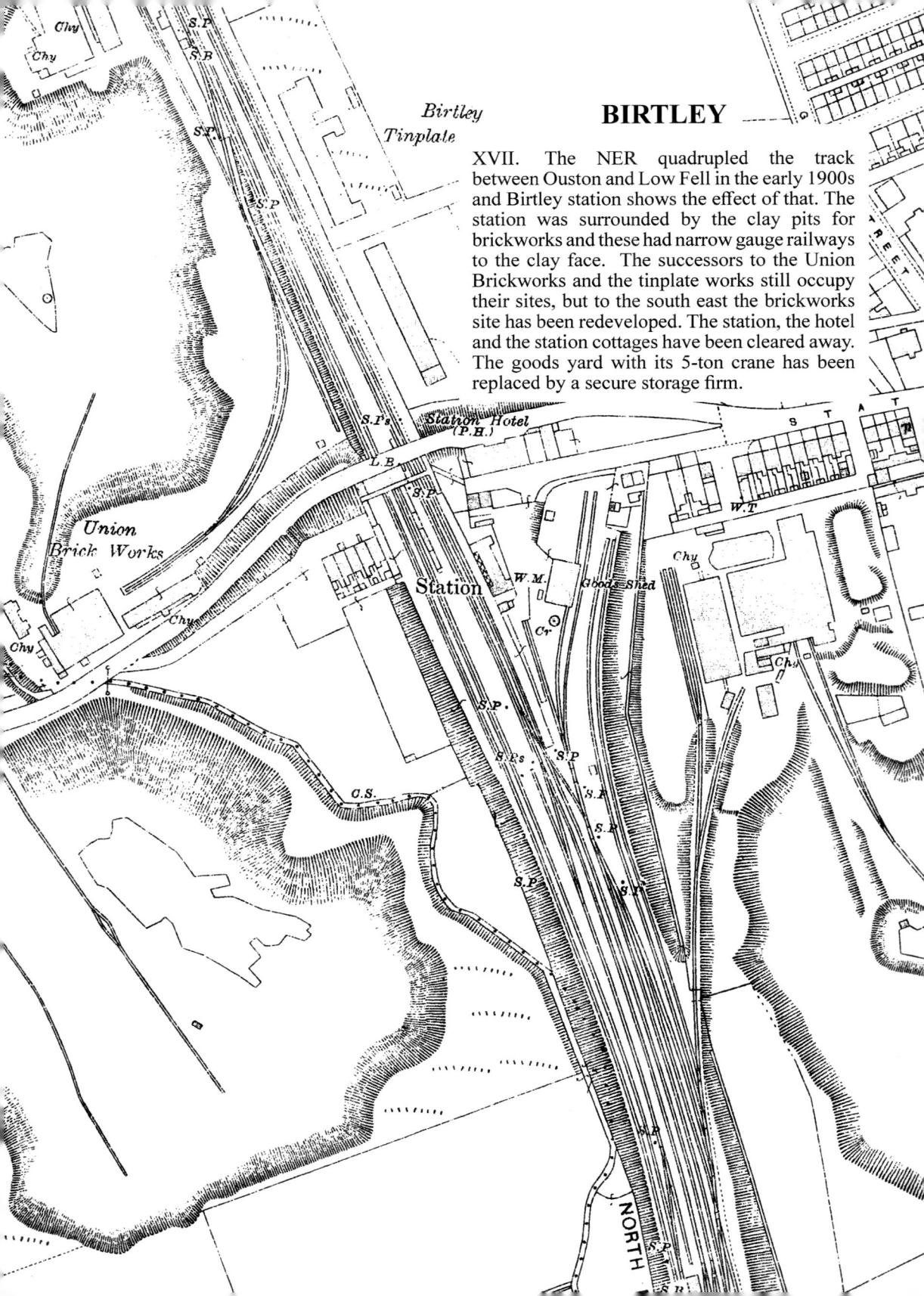

84. Birtley station in 1890 had the same overall design as Chester-le-Street, but with a slightly different central roof line. The signal box controls the level crossing and station signals with signal rodding by the platform and between the tracks. The staff pose for the photographer before the days of Health and Safety directives. (Beamish Museum)

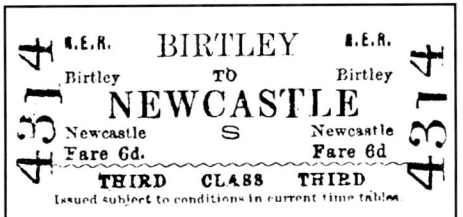

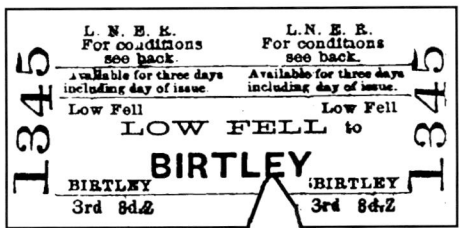

↑ 85. By 1910 the tracks had been quadrupled with extra platform faces. A bridge replaced the level crossing and the roofline of the Station Hotel appears behind the station. The ticket office is on the bridge over the new tracks. In the first half of the twentieth century the population doubled to nearly 11,000 and competing bus services improved. The station remained basically the same until its closure on 5th December 1955. (Stations UK)

← 86. In this aerial view of the tinplate works the station is on the right hand edge. Behind the goods yard is the Station Brickworks with its flooded clay pit. One interesting detail is the regularly spaced and neatly clipped bushes with white chipping gravel beds lining the tracks. In the 1930s, John Millar, the LNER Chief Area Engineer, believed that an attractive lineside was an important contribution to the pleasure of a journey. Would that this was part of today's philosophy!
(Beamish Museum)

87. On 25th July 2006, no. 66132 was going north with an EWS coal train through the station site. The tracks are reduced to two once more. On the left is the storage firm on the goods yard site and in the background is the Komat'su UK Ltd plant, successors to the Caterpillar factory. Rail traffic to the site ceased in 1966, but Komat'su have an internal siding on which they test their road/rail vehicles. (R.R.Darsley)

88. From 1915 to 1918, with the Ministry of Munitions complex at Birtley was a National Projectile factory employing 4000 Belgian workers under the control of the Belgian government. The workers lived in an enclosed village nearby, named Elisabeth. The factory locomotive no.9 was also unusual. It was built for the South Devon Railway by Avonside (their no.1055 of 1874), as a broad gauge (7ft.0in.) engine called *Lark*. It was rebuilt to standard gauge in 1892 as GWR no.1332 and later sold to industry. At Birtley it was joined by similar locomotives, no. 8 and no.10, originally SDR *Crow* and *Jay*, respectively. (D.G.Charlton)

TYNE YARD

89. This view of Tyne Yard under construction was taken from the lighting tower at the south end of the complex on 31st May 1963. It shows the shunting hump with its retarders, the control tower and the fan of sidings. The ECML is to the far right, behind the control tower. In 2006 the tower was intact but mothballed. (BR/K.Hoole coll.)

➜ 90. The intrepid photographer climbed another lighting tower to take this south facing view of the sidings on 9th July 1963. The ECML is on the left and the flyover giving access from the up line is also visible. Many of the tracks have gone but the northern end of the yard is still in use. The Tyne Yard joins the ECML on the site of Lamesley station. (BR/K.Hoole coll.)

➜ 91. At the northern end of the yard is the EWS office block, wagon and locomotive maintenance shed. It was used primarily to stage coal and departmental service trains and had a virtual ballast quarry. It sees coal, oil, steel and alumina trains, also Nissan car trains to Italy via the Channel Tunnel. There is also a stabling and servicing point for Virgin Voyagers. In the foreground no. 66116 uncouples from its train of EWS box cars on 25th July 2006. (R.R.Darsley)

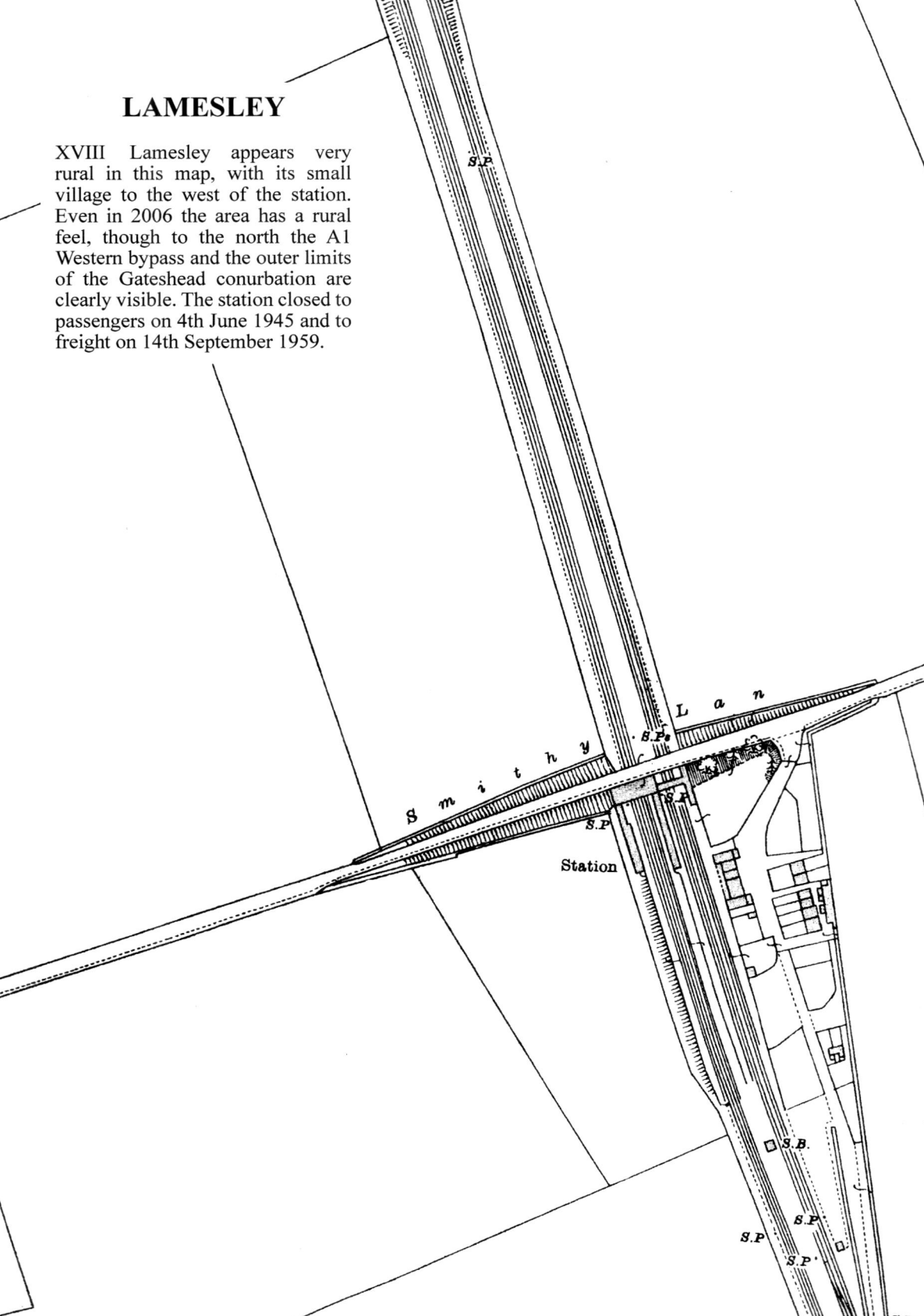

LAMESLEY

XVIII Lamesley appears very rural in this map, with its small village to the west of the station. Even in 2006 the area has a rural feel, though to the north the A1 Western bypass and the outer limits of the Gateshead conurbation are clearly visible. The station closed to passengers on 4th June 1945 and to freight on 14th September 1959.

92. The station was to the same style as Birtley, both in the original design and in the rebuilding when the tracks were quadrupled. The ticket office was built on the roadbridge. In this 1912 photograph, a NER stopping train to Newcastle was just leaving the station. (Lens of Sutton coll.)

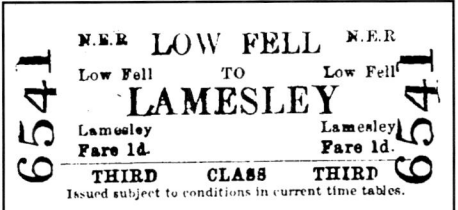

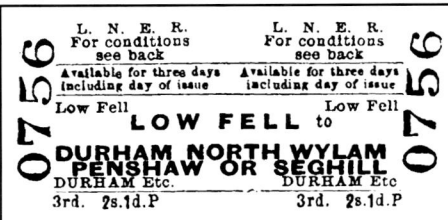

93. The station has closed and the platforms are overgrown, though the platform facings are intact. The signal box was still in use on 6th June 1960, as class K1 2-6-0 no.62030 hauls a train of mineral empties on the widened lines. (Milepost 92½)

94. The site was completely altered by the building of the Tyne Yard. No. 40040 is passing with a down passenger train on 28th August 1974. The new bridge is still a popular vantage point. The freight stock shows interesting changes. There is a typical 1960s mixed freight and a fitted van train that no longer required a guards van. Trainload freight is in evidence with two trains of tank wagons and there is a short container train. (T.Heavyside)

LOW FELL

XIX. The four tracks continued north through Low Fell station as far as the junction for Dunston. The station was in pleasant suburban surroundings, for Low Fell was, and still is, a superior part of Gateshead. The station had a coal depot, but not a freight yard. Passenger services ceased on 7th April 1952. Though the station buildings have gone, there are remnants of the up platform and three railway cottages have been modernised to make two houses.

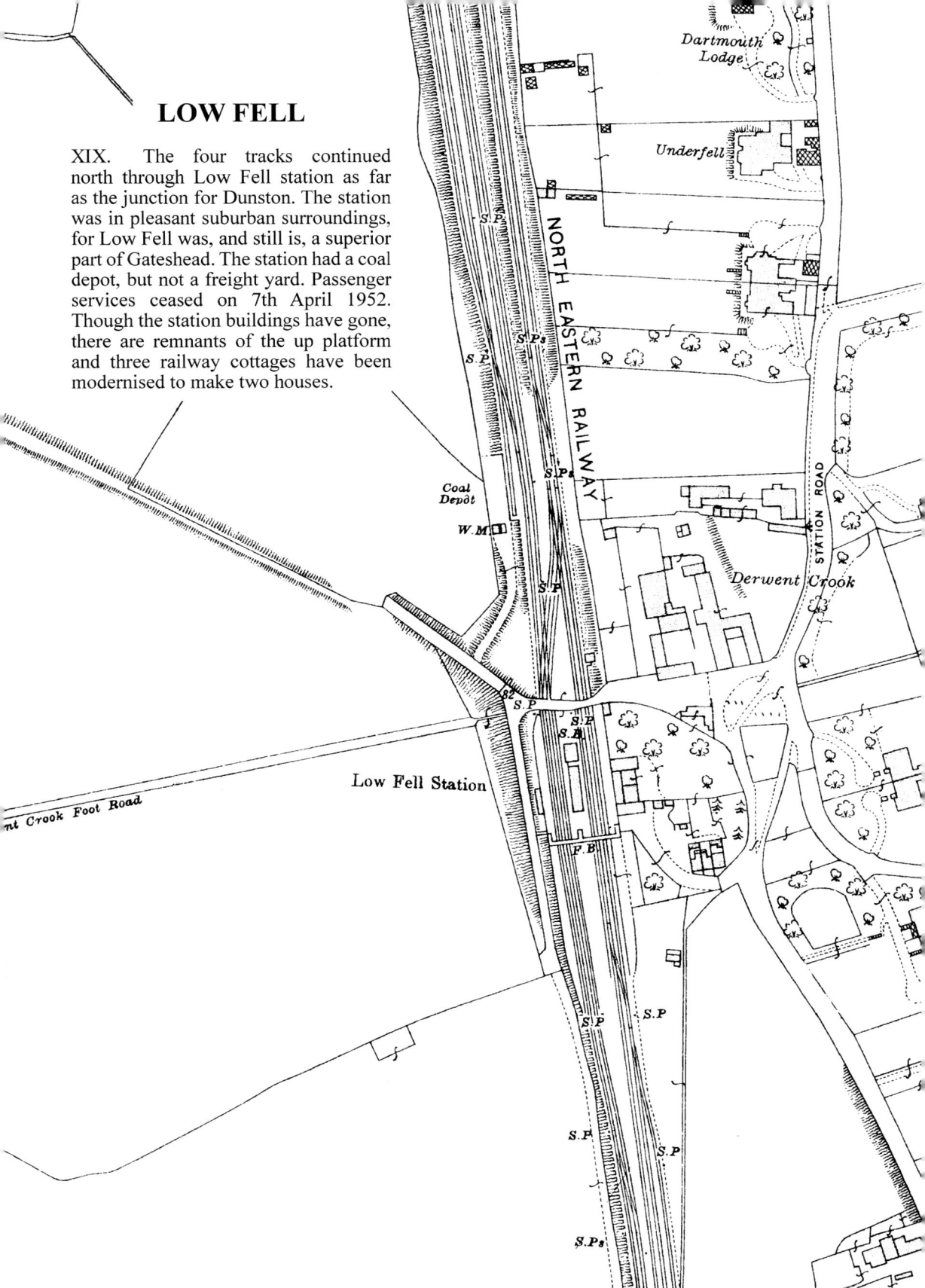

95. The station follows the style we have seen from Chester-le-Street northwards. Even though there was a convenient road bridge, the original station buildings continued to be used as the ticket office when the line was quadrupled. The four platforms were connected by two NER footbridges. A freight train is seen disappearing north with a NER clerestory guards van on the rear.
(Beamish Museum)

96. NER 2-4-0 no.1448 is on an up passenger train. The 1440 class was Edward Fletcher's last design and was a small wheeled version of his famous 901 class. Of the 15 locomotives built between 1876 and 1882, nine passed into LNER ownership. (K.Nunn/Beamish coll.)

97. Two of Vincent Raven's Atlantics (NER Z class, later C7) head north from the station with an express in conditions of icy snow. (B.Greenfield/ NELPG coll.)

98. The signal box still commands the scene, as class Q6 0-8-0 no. 63363 trundles south through the station on the goods lines in May 1956. The station house remained intact until the stationmaster's widow died. It was then used as a mess room and store until electrification was completed and it was then demolished. (J.W.Armstrong Trust)

99. North of the station, Low Fell Junction had a west curve towards Dunston. This was electrified as far as the Royal Mail Tyneside Automated Mail Centre. Here no. 47772 and no. 90020 *Colonel Bill Cockburn CBE TD* take the first departure, the 14.06 London mail train, up the bank from the depot on 6th March 1995. Mail trains also used class 86 and class 325 parcel EMUs. In the background is the Low Fell storeyard. This permanent way yard was where the famous Newcastle east end diamond crossings were assembled. (R.Lumley)

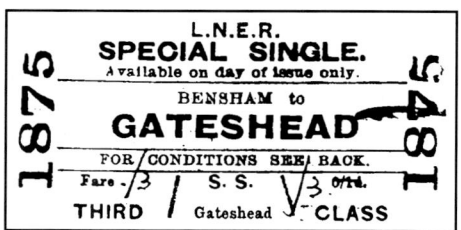

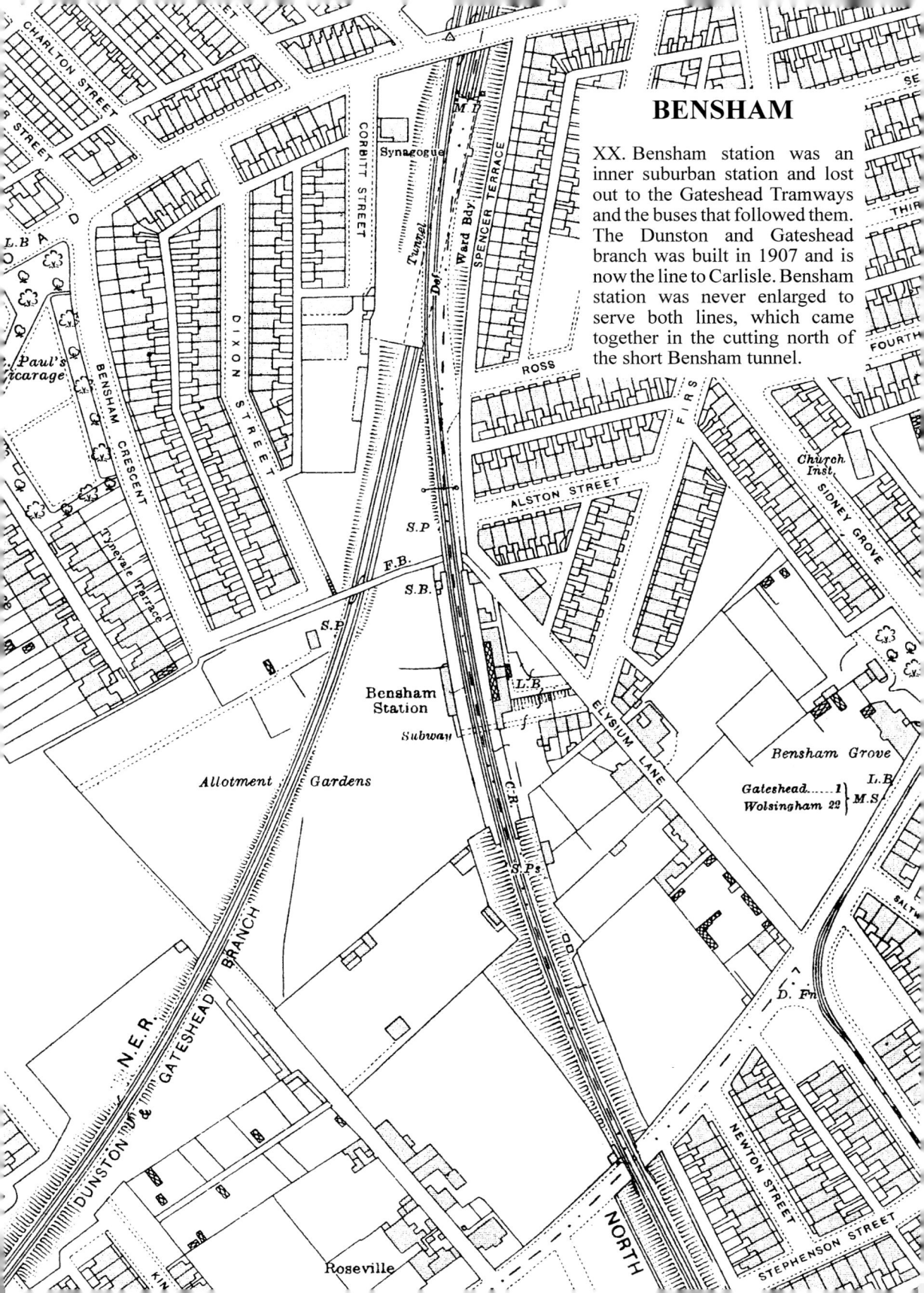

BENSHAM

XX. Bensham station was an inner suburban station and lost out to the Gateshead Tramways and the buses that followed them. The Dunston and Gateshead branch was built in 1907 and is now the line to Carlisle. Bensham station was never enlarged to serve both lines, which came together in the cutting north of the short Bensham tunnel.

100. The station had brick buildings with wooden platforms. The main building was on the upside and had large glass verandas. There was no footbridge but the 'Way Out' sign led to a subway. There was another underpass beyond the signal box. The staff are posed in this 1912 photograph, with the stationmaster in the foreground to the right. (Lens of Sutton coll.)

101. The station closed on 5th April 1954 and by the end of the 1950s the wooden platforms had been removed. The main building has been let to a business, though there is still a NER lamp on the wall by the 'Enquiries' sign. A remnant of the veranda remains. (Stations UK)

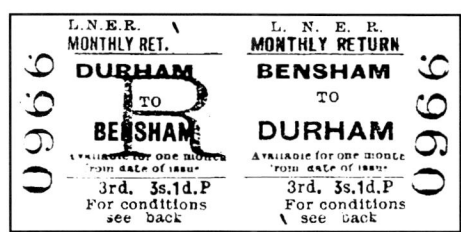

102. The station has completely disappeared. No. 91105 *County Durham* is heading for Newcastle, as it passes through the site on 18th July 2006. The photographer was on the retaining wall of the underpass to take this view. The up side of the site is a Gateshead Council Butterfly Park, but it was rather neglected. (R.R.Darsley)

GATESHEAD WEST

XXI. The map shows the King Edward Bridge junction with most of the bridge, the Gateshead works and locomotive shed and the Gateshead stations, West and East. The lines at the top run to the High Level Bridge. Riversdale Road led to the original Newcastle and Carlisle Railway Redheugh station on the river bank. The connecting incline has had its tracks removed. The road now leads to the Tyneside Integrated Electronic Control Centre that signals the tracks from Darlington through Newcastle to Morpeth.

For further photographs of Gateshead see the *Newcastle to Hexham* album, photograph nos 13-17.

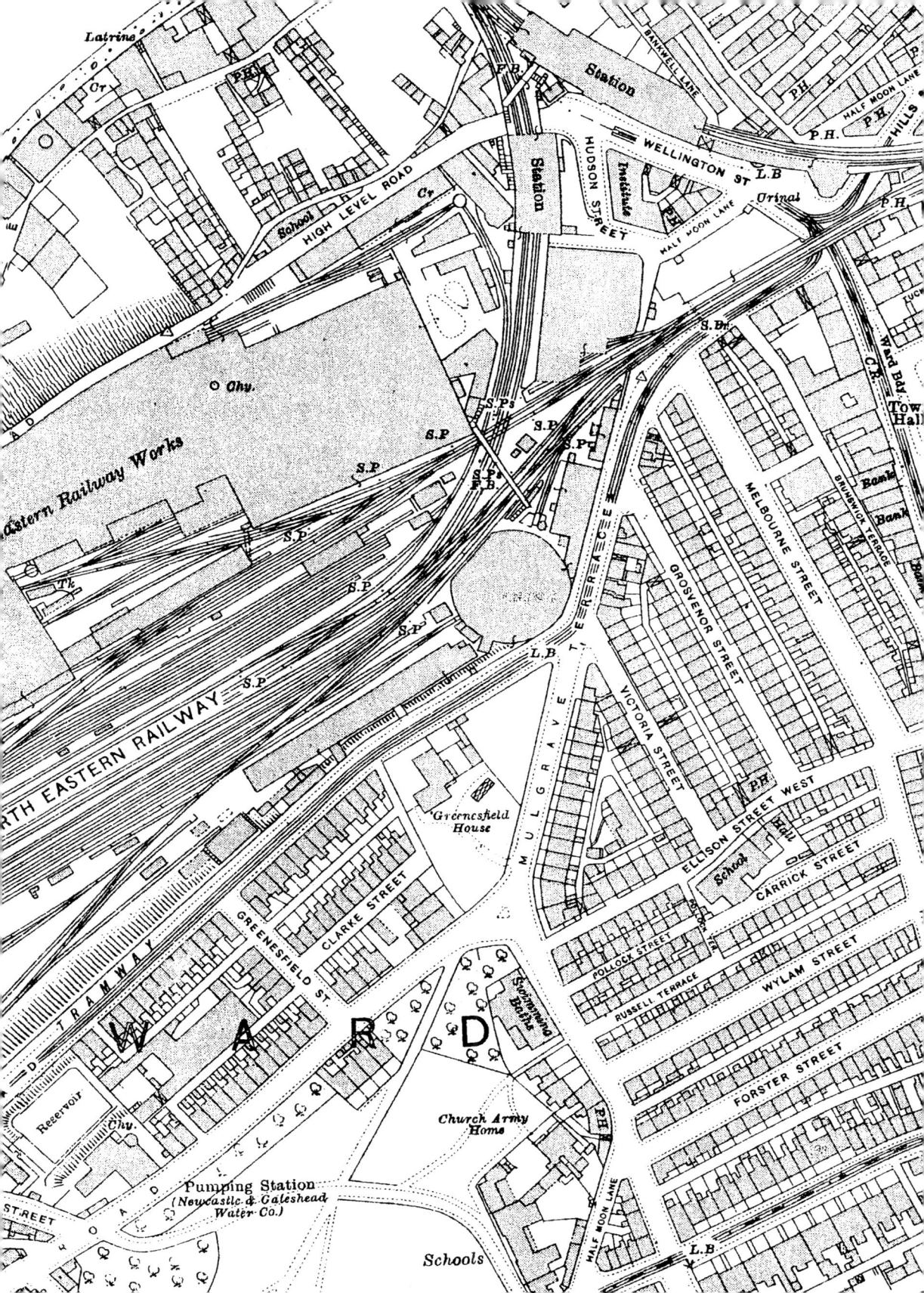

103. Prior to 1907 all trains arrived at or departed from Newcastle Central via the High Level Bridge. In 1907, the 462 yd. King Edward VII bridge was opened giving a flexible circuit between Gateshead and Newcastle. Class A3 4-6-2 no. 60084 *Trigo* is coming off the King Edward VII bridge with the "Queen of Scots" Pullman train in this 1950s photograph. (R.S.Carpenter)

104. In 1963 Type 4 no. D273 is heading south with a train for Liverpool having come from Newcastle via the High Level Bridge and Gateshead West. In the background is Gateshead shed (coded 52A) and works. The rather decayed terrace houses have been demolished, as have their high rise concrete replacements. (I.Patterson)

105. Gateshead steam depot contained four round houses, three of them under the same roof. In its gloomy interior are A1, A2 and A3 Pacifics, a V2 2-6-2 and three B1 4-6-0s. Two enginemen are manoeuvring the turntable to allow a locomotive to leave. (K.Hoole coll.)

106. Gateshead shed was modernised for the maintenance of diesel locomotives. This panoramic view of Gateshead diesel depot also shows the double deck High Level Bridge, Armstrong's swing bridge and the iconic Tyne Bridge. (G.Peacock/R.R.Darsley coll.)

107. A fair selection of Gateshead's allocation on 25th August 1972 is shown here. From left to right, there are two class 47s, class O3 0-6-0DM no. 2156, class 55 Co-CoDE no. 9011 *The Royal Northumberland Fusiliers*, class 46 1-Co-Co-1DE no.183, class 40 1-Co-Co-1DE no.358 and finally another class 47, no.1518. (T.Heavyside)

108. All the Gateshead sheds and works have been swept away by the Ochre Yard residential and office development. Freightliner no. 66621 hauls the Oxwellmains to Seaham cement train towards Gateshead West junction on 18th July 2006. Passenger trains sometimes use this route to approach Newcastle Central or to turn sets around. (R.R.Darsley)

109. The station looked rather desolate even in the 1930s for it lost its purpose when the King Edward VII bridge opened and the Dunston passenger shuttle ceased in 1926. In 2006 only the station platforms remained and the approach to the High Level Bridge had been singled. The up platform is isolated and trackless but the down platform is still accessible. (Lens of Sutton coll.)

110. Class K1 2-6-0 no.2005 with an excursion train crossed the High Level bridge 112 ft. above high water on 17th April 1986. In the background is Gateshead works and the site of Gateshead West station. The tracks on the 150 year old bridge have since been reduced to two. In 2005 the 330 yd. bridge was closed to road traffic for repairs to the cast iron work. The work needed was more major than expected and the roadway will be closed until 2008. (D.Trevor Rowe)

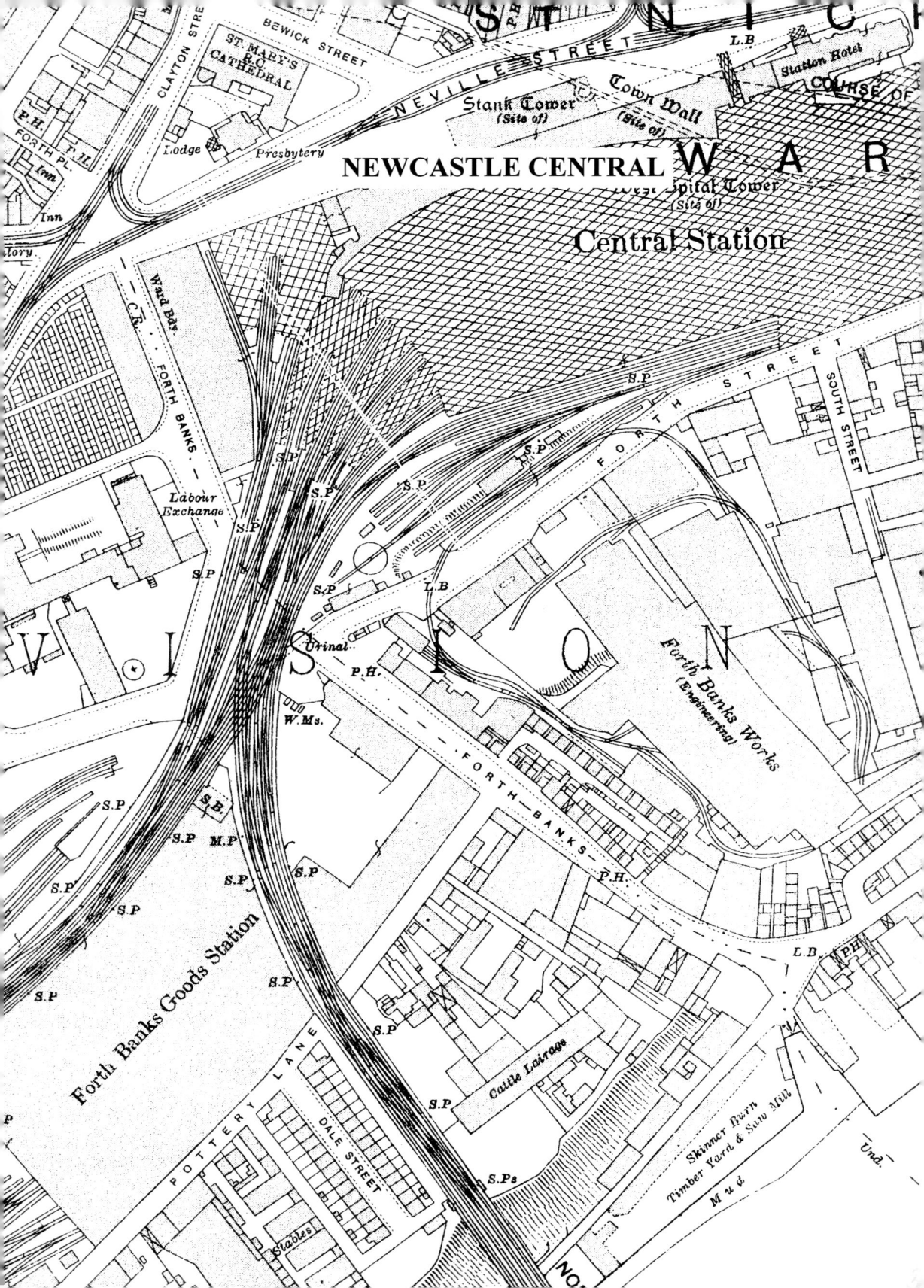

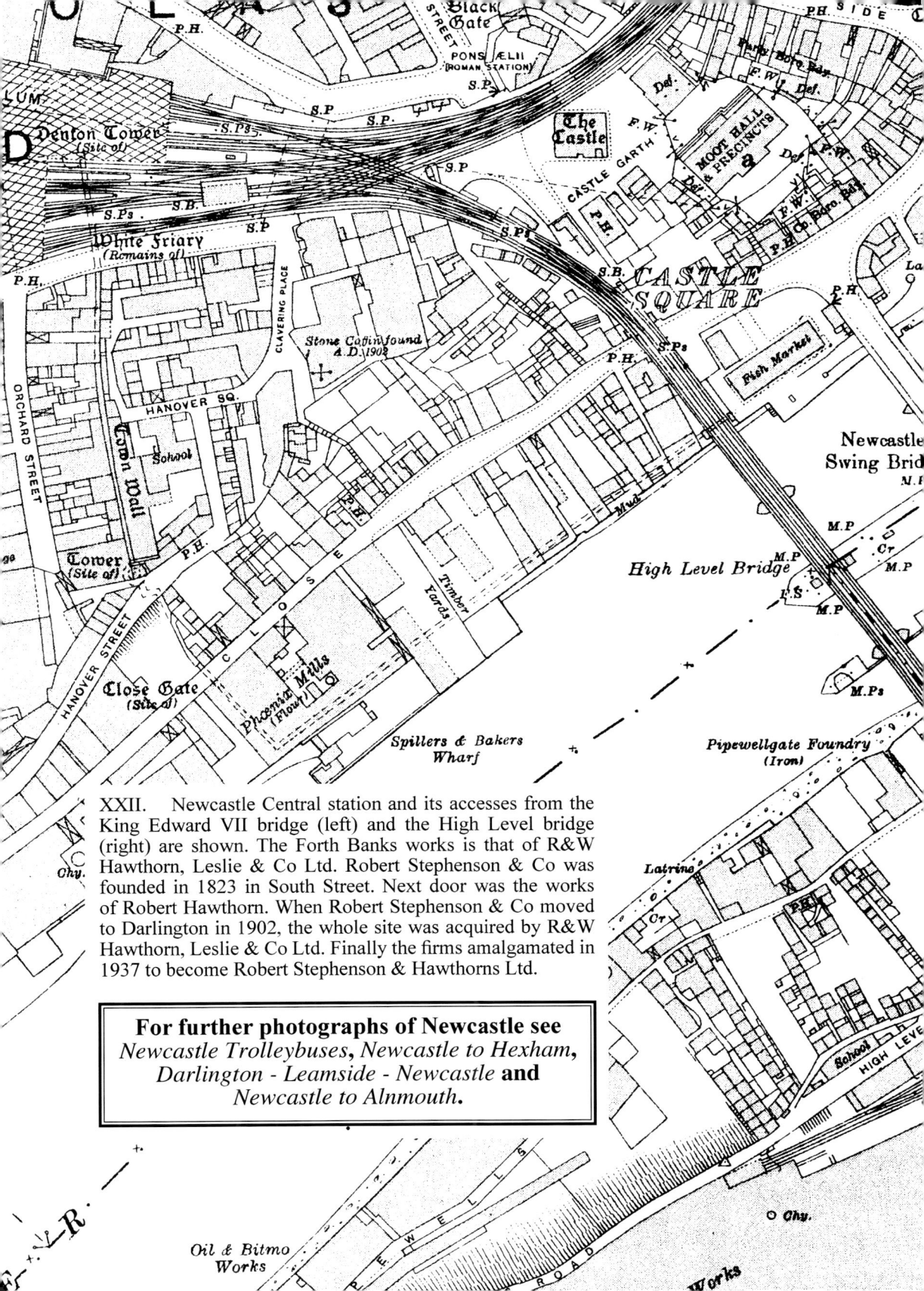

XXII. Newcastle Central station and its accesses from the King Edward VII bridge (left) and the High Level bridge (right) are shown. The Forth Banks works is that of R&W Hawthorn, Leslie & Co Ltd. Robert Stephenson & Co was founded in 1823 in South Street. Next door was the works of Robert Hawthorn. When Robert Stephenson & Co moved to Darlington in 1902, the whole site was acquired by R&W Hawthorn, Leslie & Co Ltd. Finally the firms amalgamated in 1937 to become Robert Stephenson & Hawthorns Ltd.

For further photographs of Newcastle see
Newcastle Trolleybuses, Newcastle to Hexham, Darlington - Leamside - Newcastle **and** *Newcastle to Alnmouth.*

111. Our route from Darlington to Newcastle ends at the west end of Newcastle Central station. In 1938 the platforms were guarded by a fine array of signals. This photograph was taken from No.3 signal box. Class A3 4-6-2 no. 2596 *Manna* makes its way, light engine, across King Edward VII bridge to Gateshead shed. Behind the building carrying the OXO advert is the start of the steep sidings leading down to the Forth Banks works. (Stations UK)

Robert Stephenson & Hawthorns Ltd
(Forth Banks)

112. It was at Forth Banks, in his new locomotive works, that Robert Stephenson with his father, George, built *Rocket*. Both his works and Hawthorns next door had internal railway systems but were not connected to the NER until 1893. *Rocket* went by road to Carlisle and then by sea to Liverpool. This view of Stephenson's South Street works entrance includes one of the road wagons used for carrying parts of finished locomotives. The wagon had horses in the two sets of shafts and six more in traces. (McDowell Trust coll./SLS)

113. This was the final line up of locomotives in the erecting shop at South Street before Robert Stephenson & Co moved to Darlington in 1902. After the last amalgamation in 1937, the Forth Banks works was generally used for industrial locomotive orders, while the Darlington works built the mainline locomotives. The exception was the construction of GWR 0-6-0PT nos. 9410-89 built between 1950 and 1953. No. 9466 from this batch is currently preserved at the Buckinghamshire Railway Centre. The works closed in 1960. (McDowell Trust coll./SLS)

114. This is a photograph posed by the firm at the interchange of their sidings with the main line. Newcastle Central station is on the left. There are two crane tanks, the nearest named *Hawthorn*. The safety of the shunter does not appear to be a consideration. Hawthorn Leslie designed crane tanks which were popular in the local shipyards. *Hawthorn*, their no. 2768 of 1909, was sold to Armstrong Whitworth & Co for their Elswick Works. (R.Stephenson Trust)

115. Newcastle Central station was designed by John Dobson and built in 1850, but the portico was not completed until 1861. It is seen in the 1950s, when the Maynard's sweets kiosk was open for business. Newcastle Corporation trolleybuses and buses in their distinctive yellow and cream livery are in Neville Street. The former are featured in a Middleton Press album, *Newcastle Trolleybuses*. (Rev.J.Parker)

116. The main concourse of the station was crowded in a 1950s rush hour. Passengers have cardboard suitcases and can take their bicycles on the train. Baths are available for gentlemen; were there equivalent facilities for ladies? (Rev.J.Parker)

117. The most favoured spot for photographers was the west end of Newcastle Central main line platforms and this fine study shows A3 4-6-2 no. 60077 *The White Knight* leaving for Kings Cross on 11th April 1955. (R.Leslie)

118. Although so many prints from this position are available, this one is a little more unusual. The first GWR Castle class to arrive at Newcastle was 4-6-0 no. 7029 *Clun Castle*. It was working the return excursion to King's Cross on Sunday 10th September 1967. Keen observers will note that the engine has not yet been coupled. It had backed down until the cylinder clearance was 1/16 in. from the platform. The carriages were then brought up to the engine from the rear. (A.C.Clothier)

119. Our train from Darlington has arrived at platform 8 with no. 47458 on Sunday 27th August 1978. Refurbishment of the interior in 1989 not only led to platform renumbering, but to a new glass and steel travel centre. (T.Heavyside)

120. Some of the franchises operating in Newcastle in 2005 are represented by trains in this photograph. They are Arriva Northern no. 142071, Strathclyde Passenger Transport no. 156505 on the Carlisle route, GNER no. 82220 en route to Edinburgh and Virgin Trains no.220021 *Staffordshire Voyager* waiting to depart south. The date is 22nd August. (R.R.Darsley)

EVOLVING THE
Vic Mitchell and Keith Smith
ULTIMATE RAIL ENCYCLOPEDIA
INTERNATIONAL

126a Camelsdale Road, GU27 3RJ. Tel:01730 813169

A-978 0 906520 B- 978 1 873793 C- 978 1 901706 D-978 1 904474
E - 978 1 906008 F - 978 1 908174 G - 978 1 910356

Our RAILWAY titles are listed below. Please check availability by looking at our website **www.middletonpress.co.uk,** telephoning us or by requesting a Brochure which includes our LATEST RAILWAY TITLES also our TRAMWAY, TROLLEYBUS, MILITARY and COASTAL series.

email:info@middletonpress.co.uk

A
Abergavenny to Merthyr C 91 8
Abertillery & Ebbw Vale Lines D 84 5
Aberystwyth to Carmarthen E 90 1
Alnmouth to Berwick G 50 0
Alton - Branch Lines to A 11 6
Ambergate to Buxton G 28 9
Ambergate to Mansfield G 39 5
Andover to Southampton A 82 6
Ascot - Branch Lines around A 64 2
Ashburton - Branch Line to B 95 4
Ashford - Steam to Eurostar B 67 1
Ashford to Dover A 48 2
Austrian Narrow Gauge D 04 3
Avonmouth - BL around D 42 5
Aylesbury to Rugby D 91 3

B
Baker Street to Uxbridge D 90 6
Bala to Llandudno E 87 1
Banbury to Birmingham D 27 2
Banbury to Cheltenham E 63 5
Bangor to Holyhead F 01 7
Bangor to Portmadoc E 72 7
Barking to Southend C 80 2
Barmouth to Pwllheli E 53 6
Barry - Branch Lines around D 50 0
Bartlow - Branch Lines to F 27 7
Basingstoke to Salisbury A 89 4
Bath Green Park to Bristol C 36 9
Bath to Evercreech Junction A 60 4
Beamish 40 years on rails E94 9
Bedford to Wellingborough D 31 9
Berwick to Drem F 64 2
Berwick to St. Boswells F 75 8
B'ham to Tamworth & Nuneaton F 63 5
Birkenhead to West Kirby F 61 1
Birmingham to Wolverhampton E253
Blackburn to Hellifield F 95 6
Bletchley to Cambridge D 94 4
Bletchley to Rugby E 07 9
Bodmin - Branch Lines around B 83 1
Bolton to Preston G 61 6
Boston to Lincoln F 80 2
Bournemouth to Evercreech Jn A 46 8
Bradshaw's History F18 5
Bradshaw's Rail Times 1850 F 13 0
Branch Lines series - see town names
Brecon to Neath D 43 2
Brecon to Newport D 16 6
Brecon to Newtown E 06 2
Brighton to Eastbourne A 16 1
Brighton to Worthing A 03 1
Bristol to Taunton D 03 6
Bromley South to Rochester B 23 7
Bromsgrove to Birmingham D 87 6
Bromsgrove to Gloucester D 73 9
Broxbourne to Cambridge F16 1
Brunel - A railtour D 74 6
Bude - Branch Line to B 29 9
Burnham to Evercreech Jn B 68 0
Buxton to Stockport G 32 6

C
Cambridge to Ely D 55 5
Canterbury - BLs around B 58 9
Cardiff to Dowlais (Cae Harris) E 47 5
Cardiff to Pontypridd E 95 6
Cardiff to Swansea E 42 0
Carlisle to Beattock G 69 2
Carlisle to Hawick E 85 7
Carmarthen to Fishguard E 66 6
Caterham & Tattenham Corner B251
Central & Southern Spain NG E 91 8
Chard and Yeovil - BLs a C 30 7
Charing Cross to Orpington A 96 3
Cheddar - Branch Line to B 90 9
Cheltenham to Andover C 43 7
Cheltenham to Redditch D 81 4
Chesterfield to Lincoln G 21 0
Chester to Birkenhead F 21 5
Chester to Manchester F 51 2
Chester to Rhyl E 93 2
Chester to Warrington F 40 6
Chichester to Portsmouth A 14 7
Clacton and Walton - BLs to F 04 8
Clapham Jn to Beckenham Jn B 36 7
Cleobury Mortimer - BLs a E 18 5
Clevedon & Portishead - BLs to D180
Consett to South Shields E 57 4
Cornwall Narrow Gauge D 56 2
Corris and Vale of Rheidol E 65 9
Coventry to Leicester G 00 5
Craven Arms to Llandeilo E 35 2
Craven Arms to Wellington E 33 8
Crawley to Littlehampton A 34 5
Crewe to Manchester F 57 4
Crewe to Wigan G 12 8
Cromer - Branch Lines around C 26 0
Cromford and High Peak G 35 7
Croydon to East Grinstead B 48 0
Crystal Palace & Catford Loop B 87 1
Cyprus Narrow Gauge E 13 0

D
Darjeeling Revisited F 09 3
Darlington Leamside Newcastle E 28 4
Darlington to Newcastle D 98 2
Dartford to Sittingbourne B 34 3
Denbigh - Branch Lines around F 32 1
Derby to Chesterfield G 11 1
Derby to Nottingham G 45 6
Derby to Stoke-on-Trent F 93 2
Derwent Valley - BL to the D 06 7
Devon Narrow Gauge E 09 3
Didcot to Banbury D 02 9
Didcot to Swindon C 84 0
Didcot to Winchester C 13 0
Diss to Norwich G 22 7
Dorset & Somerset NG D 76 0
Douglas - Laxey - Ramsey E 75 8
Douglas to Peel C 88 8
Douglas to Port Erin C 55 0
Douglas to Ramsey D 39 5
Dover to Ramsgate A 78 9
Drem to Edinburgh G 06 7
Dublin Northwards in 1950s E 31 4
Dunstable - Branch Lines to E 27 7

E
Ealing to Slough C 42 0
Eastbourne to Hastings A 27 7
East Croydon to Three Bridges A 53 6
Eastern Spain Narrow Gauge E 56 7
East Grinstead - BLs to A 07 9
East Kent Light Railway A 61 1
East London - Branch Lines of C 44 4
East London Line B 80 0
East of Norwich - Branch Lines E 69 7
Effingham Junction - BLs a A 74 1
Ely to Norwich C 90 1
Enfield Town & Palace Gates D 32 6
Epsom to Horsham A 30 7
Eritrean Narrow Gauge E 38 3
Euston to Harrow & Wealdstone C 89 5
Exeter to Barnstaple B 15 2
Exeter to Newton Abbot C 49 9
Exeter to Tavistock B 69 5
Exmouth - Branch Lines to B 00 8

F
Fairford - Branch Line to A 52 9
Falmouth, Helston & St. Ives C 74 1
Fareham to Salisbury A 67 3
Faversham to Dover B 05 3
Felixstowe & Aldeburgh - BL to D 20 3
Fenchurch Street to Barking C 20 8
Festiniog - 50 yrs of enterprise C 83 3
Festiniog 1946-55 E 01 7
Festiniog in the Fifties B 68 8
Festiniog in the Sixties B 91 6
Ffestiniog in Colour 1955-82 F 25 3
Finsbury Park to Alexandra Pal C 02 8
French Metre Gauge Survivors F 88 8
Frome to Bristol B 77 0

G
Gainsborough to Sheffield G 17 3
Galashiels to Edinburgh F 52 9
Gloucester to Bristol D 35 7
Gloucester to Cardiff D 66 1
Gosport - Branch Lines around A 36 9
Greece Narrow Gauge D 72 2
Guildford to Redhill A 63 5

H
Hampshire Narrow Gauge D 36 4
Harrow to Watford D 14 2
Harwich & Hadleigh - BLs to F 02 4
Harz Revisited F 62 8
Hastings to Ashford A 37 6
Hawick to Galashiels F 36 9
Hawkhurst - Branch Line to A 66 6
Hayling - Branch Line to A 12 3
Hay-on-Wye - BL around D 92 0
Haywards Heath to Seaford A 28 4
Hemel Hempstead - BLs to D 88 3
Henley, Windsor & Marlow - BLa C77 2
Hereford to Newport D 54 8
Hertford & Hatfield - BLs a E 58 1
Hertford Loop E 71 0
Hexham to Carlisle D 75 3
Hexham to Hawick F 08 6
Hitchin to Peterborough D 07 4
Horsham - Branch Lines to A 02 4
Hull, Hornsea and Withernsea G 27 2
Hull to Scarborough G 60 9
Huntingdon - Branch Line to A 93 2

I
Ilford to Shenfield C 97 0
Ilfracombe - Branch Line to B 21 3
Ilkeston to Chesterfield G 26 5
Inverkeithing to Thornton Jct G 76 0
Ipswich to Diss F 81 9
Ipswich to Saxmundham C 41 3
Isle of Man Railway Journey F 94 9
Isle of Wight Lines - 50 yrs C 12 3
Italy Narrow Gauge F 17 8

K
Kent Narrow Gauge C 45 1
Kettering to Nottingham F 82-6
Kidderminster to Shrewsbury E 10 9
Kingsbridge - Branch Line to C 98 7
Kings Cross to Potters Bar E 62 8
King's Lynn to Hunstanton F 58 1
Kingston & Hounslow Loops A 83 3
Kingswear - Branch Line to C 17 8

L
Lambourn - Branch Line to C 70 3
Lancaster to Oxenholme G 77 7
Launceston & Princetown - BLs C 19 2
Leeds to Selby G 47 0
Leek - Branch Line From G 01 2
Leicester to Burton F 85 7
Leicester to Nottingham G 15 9
Lewisham to Dartford A 92 5
Lincoln to Cleethorpes F 56 7
Lincoln to Doncaster G 03 6
Lines around Newmarket G 54 8
Lines around Stamford F 98 7
Lines around Wimbledon B 75 6
Lines North of Stoke G 29 6
Liverpool to Runcorn G 72 2
Liverpool Street to Chingford D 01 2
Liverpool Street to Ilford C 34 5
Llandeilo to Swansea E 46 8
London Bridge to Addiscombe B 20 6
London Bridge to East Croydon A 58 1
Longmoor - Branch Lines to A 41 3
Looe - Branch Line to C 22 2
Loughborough to Ilkeston G 24 1
Loughborough to Nottingham F 68 0
Lowestoft - BLs around E 40 6
Ludlow to Hereford E 14 7
Lydney - Branch Lines around E 26 0
Lyme Regis - Branch Line to A 45 1
Lynton - Branch Line to B 04 6

M
Machynlleth to Barmouth E 54 3
Maesteg and Tondu Lines F 06 2
Majorca & Corsica Narrow Gauge F 41 3
Manchester to Bacup G 46 3
Mansfield to Doncaster G 23 4
March - Branch Lines around B 09 1
Market Drayton - BLs around F 67 3
Market Harborough to Newark F 86 4
Marylebone to Rickmansworth D 49 4
Melton Constable to Yarmouth Bch E031
Midhurst - Branch Lines of E 78 9
Midhurst - Branch Lines to F 00 0
Minehead - Branch Line to A 80 2
Monmouth - Branch Lines to E 20 8
Monmouthshire Eastern Valleys D 71 5
Moretonhampstead - BL to C 27 7
Moreton-in-Marsh to Worcester D 26 5
Morpeth to Bellingham F 87 1
Mountain Ash to Neath D 80 7

N
Newark to Doncaster F 78 9
Newbury to Westbury C 66 6
Newcastle to Alnmouth G 36 4
Newcastle to Hexham D 69 2
Newmarket to Haughley & Laxfield G 71 5
New Mills to Sheffield G 44 9
Newport (IOW) - Branch Lines to A 26 0
Newquay - Branch Lines to C 71 0
Newton Abbot to Plymouth C 60 4
Newtown to Aberystwyth E 41 3
Northampton to Peterborough F 92 5
North East German NG D 44 9
Northern Alpine Narrow Gauge F 37 6
Northern Spain Narrow Gauge E 83 3
North London Line B 94 7
North of Birmingham F 55 0
North of Grimsby - Branch Lines G 09 8
North Woolwich - BLs around C 65 9
Nottingham to Boston F 70 3
Nottingham to Kirkby Bentinck G 38 8
Nottingham to Lincoln F 43 7
Nottingham to Mansfield G 52 4
Nuneaton to Loughborough G 08 1

O
Ongar - Branch Line to E 05 5
Orpington to Tonbridge B 03 9
Oswestry - Branch Lines around E 60 4
Oswestry to Whitchurch E 81 9
Oxford to Bletchley D 57 9
Oxford to Moreton-in-Marsh D 15 9

P
Paddington to Ealing C 37 6
Paddington to Princes Risborough C819
Padstow - Branch Line to B 54 1
Peebles Loop G 19 7
Pembroke and Cardigan - BLs to F 29 1
Peterborough to Kings Lynn E 32 1
Peterborough to Lincoln F 89 5
Peterborough to Newark F 72 7
Plymouth - BLs around B 98 5
Plymouth to St. Austell C 63 5
Pontypool to Mountain Ash D 65 4
Pontypridd to Merthyr F 14 7
Pontypridd to Port Talbot E 86 4
Porthmadog 1954-94 - BLa B 31 2
Portmadoc 1923-46 - BLa B 13 8
Portsmouth to Southampton A 31 4
Portugal Narrow Gauge E 67 3
Potters Bar to Cambridge D 70 8
Preston to Blackpool G 16 6
Preston to the Fylde Coast G 81 4
Preston to Lancaster G 74 6
Princes Risborough - BL to D 05 0
Princes Risborough to Banbury C 85 7

R
Railways to Victory C 16 1
Reading to Basingstoke B 27 5
Reading to Didcot C 79 6
Reading to Guildford A 47 5
Redhill to Ashford A 73 4
Return to Blaenau 1970-82 C 64 2
Rhyl to Bangor F 15 4
Rhymney & New Tredegar Lines E 48 2
Rickmansworth to Aylesbury D 61 6
Romania & Bulgaria NG E 23 9
Ross-on-Wye - BLs around E 30 7
Ruabon to Barmouth E 84 0
Rugby to Birmingham E 37 6
Rugby to Loughborough F 12 3
Rugby to Stafford F 07 9
Rugeley to Stoke-on-Trent F 90 1
Ryde to Ventnor A 19 2

S
Salisbury to Westbury B 39 8
Salisbury to Yeovil B 06 0
Sardinia and Sicily Narrow Gauge F 50 5
Saxmundham to Yarmouth C 69 7
Saxony & Baltic Germany Revisited F 71 0
Saxony Narrow Gauge D 47 0
Scunthorpe to Doncaster G 34 0
Seaton & Sidmouth - BLs to A 95 6
Selsey - Branch Line to A 04 8
Sheerness - Branch Line to B 16 2
Sheffield towards Manchester G 18 0
Shenfield to Ipswich E 96 3
Shildon to Stockton G 79 1
Shrewsbury - Branch Line to A 86 4
Shrewsbury to Chester E 70 3
Shrewsbury to Crewe F 48 2
Shrewsbury to Ludlow E 21 5
Shrewsbury to Newtown E 29 1
Sirhowy Valley Line E 12 3
Sittingbourne to Ramsgate A 90 1
Skegness & Mablethorpe - BL to F 84 0
Slough to Newbury C 56 7
South African Two-foot gauge E 51 2
Southampton to Bournemouth A 42 0
Southend & Southminster BLs E 76 5
Southern Alpine Narrow Gauge F 22 2
South London Line B 46 6
South Lynn to Norwich City F 03 1
Southwold - Branch Line to A 15 4
Spalding - Branch Lines around E 52 9
Spalding to Grimsby F 65 9 6
Stafford to Chester F 34 5
Stafford to Wellington F 59 8
St Albans to Bedford D 08 1
St. Austell to Penzance C 67 3
St. Boswell to Berwick F 44 4
Stourbridge to Wolverhampton E 16 1
St. Pancras to Barking D 68 5
St. Pancras to Folkestone E 88 8
St. Pancras to St. Albans C 78 9
Stratford to Cheshunt F 53 6
Stratford-u-Avon to Birmingham D 77 7
Stratford-u-Avon to Cheltenham C 25 3
Sudbury - Branch Lines to F 19 2
Surrey Narrow Gauge C 87 1
Sussex Narrow Gauge C 68 0
Swaffham - Branch Lines around F 97
Swanage to 1999 - BL to A 33 8
Swanley to Ashford B 45 9
Swansea - Branch Lines around F 38 3
Swansea to Carmarthen E 59 8
Swindon to Bristol C 96 3
Swindon to Gloucester D 46 3
Swindon to Newport D 30 2
Swiss Narrow Gauge C 94 9

T
Talyllyn 60 E 98 7
Tamworth to Derby F 76 5
Taunton to Barnstaple B 60 2
Taunton to Exeter C 82 6
Taunton to Minehead F 39 0
Tavistock to Plymouth B 88 6
Tenterden - Branch Line to A 21 5
Three Bridges to Brighton A 35 2
Tilbury Loop C 86 4
Tiverton - BLs around C 62 8
Tivetshall to Beccles D 41 8
Tonbridge to Hastings A 44 4
Torrington - Branch Lines to B 37 4
Tourist Railways of France G 04 3
Towcester - BLs around E 39 0
Tunbridge Wells BLs A 32 1

U
Upwell - Branch Line to B 64 0
Uttoxeter to Macclesfield G 05 0
Uttoxetor to Buxton G 33 3

V
Victoria to Bromley South A 98 7
Victoria to East Croydon A 40 6
Vivarais Revisited E 08 6

W
Walsall Routes F 45 1
Wantage - Branch Line to D 25 8
Wareham to Swanage 50 yrs D 09 8
Watercress Line G 75 3
Waterloo to Windsor A 54 3
Waterloo to Woking A 38 3
Watford to Leighton Buzzard D 45 6
Wellingborough to Leicester F 73 4
Welshpool to Llanfair E 49 9
Wenford Bridge to Fowey C 09 3
Wennington to Morecambe G 58 6
Westbury to Bath B 55 8
Westbury to Taunton C 76 5
West Cornwall Mineral Rlys D 48 7
West Croydon to Epsom B 08 4
West German Narrow Gauge D 93 7
West London - BLs of C 50 5
West London Line B 84 8
West Somerset Railway G 78 4
West Wiltshire - BLs of D 12 8
Weymouth - BLs A 65 9
Willesden Jn to Richmond B 71 8
Wimbledon to Beckenham C 58 1
Wimbledon to Epsom B 62 6
Wimborne - BLs around A 97 0
Wirksworth - Branch Lines to G 10 4
Wisbech - BLs around C 01 7
Witham & Kelvedon - BLs a E 82 6
Woking to Alton A 59 8
Woking to Portsmouth A 25 3
Woking to Southampton A 55 0
Wolverhampton to Shrewsbury E 44 4
Wolverhampton to Stafford F 79 6
Worcester to Birmingham D 97 5
Worcester to Hereford D 38 8
Worthing to Chichester A 06 2
Wrexham to New Brighton F 47 5
Wroxham - BLs around F 31 4

Y
Yeovil - 50 yrs change C 38 3
Yeovil to Dorchester A 76 5
Yeovil to Exeter A 91 8
York to Scarborough F 23 9